Security in the Nation's Capital

and the Closure of Pennsylvania Avenue: An Assessment

T0168786

Bruce Hoffman, Peter C......
with Timothy E. Liston, David W. Brannan

RAND Public Safety and Justice

This work was carried out within RAND's Public Safety and Justice Research Program under contract FCC042400. It was sponsored by the Federal City Council of the District of Columbia (FCCDC), a non-profit, nonpartisan, Washington, D.C. –based organization dedicated to the improvement of the nation's capital.

Library of Congress Cataloging-in-Publication Data

Hoffman, Bruce, 1954–
    Security in the Nation's capital and the closure of Pennsylvania Avenue : an assessment / Bruce Hoffman, Peter Chalk.
      p. cm.
    "MR-1293-1."
    Includes bibliographical references.
    ISBN 0-8330-2933-9
    1. Terrorism—Washington (D.C.)—Prevention—Evaluation. 2. White House (Washington, D.C.)—Security measures—Evaluation. 3. Presidents—Dwellings—Security measures—Washington (D.C.)—Evaluation. 4. Pennsylvania Avenue (Washington, D.C.) I. Chalk, Peter. II. Title.

HV6432 .H638 2002
363.3'2'09753—dc21

2001016076

RAND is a nonprofit institution that helps improve policy and decisionmaking through research and analysis. RAND® is a registered trademark. RAND's publications do not necessarily reflect the opinions or policies of its research sponsors.

Cover design by Maritta Tapanainen

Published 2002 by RAND
1700 Main Street, P.O. Box 2138, Santa Monica, CA 90407-2138
1200 South Hayes Street, Arlington, VA 22202-5050
201 North Craig Street, Suite 102, Pittsburgh, PA 15213-1516
RAND URL: http://www.rand.org/
To order RAND documents or to obtain additional information, contact Distribution Services: Telephone: (310) 451-7002; Fax: (310) 451-6915; Internet: order@rand.org

This assessment of ways in which Pennsylvania Avenue could be re-opened without compromising the safety and security of the President and his family or the physical integrity of the White House was completed in January 2001, before the September 11 terrorist attacks against the World Trade Center and the Pentagon. Given the enormity of the events of that day, however, it is difficult to imagine sustaining any argument except one that calls for maximum security and vigilance around the nation's most important landmarks, including the White House.

The terrorist attacks underscored the importance of examining not only alternatives that would provide security for the White House, but also more-comprehensive measures to secure all the key national landmarks in Washington, D.C. This issue was already on the national agenda: In October 2000, at the behest of the House and Senate Committees on Appropriations, the National Capital Planning Commission (NCPC) undertook an evaluation of "both Pennsylvania Avenue and more generally the impact of federal security measures on the historic urban design of Washington's Monumental Core."[1] The NCPC report, completed prior to the attacks, recommended keeping Pennsylvania Avenue closed to normal city traffic but proposed the construction of a tunnel within the Pennsylvania Avenue or E Street corridor and the use of a circulator and transportation-system management initiatives to deal with the ongoing problems inherent in blocking a major east-west traffic artery. That report thus rendered the alternatives discussed in the present study moot.

---

[1]National Capital Planning Commission, *Designing for Security in the Nation's Capital: A Report by the Interagency Task Force of the National Capital Planning Commission,* Washington, D.C., October 2001, p. 3.

However, the RAND study was not intended to propose a *specific* alternative to the closure. Its major focus was—and still is—on the importance of process in a democracy. From the start, the working assumption underlying the study was that the issue of Pennsylvania Avenue's closure was too large, too important, and too symbolically meaningful to be left in the hands of any one agency or department. When the study was undertaken in 2000, the U.S. Secret Service and the U.S. Park Service were proposing to unilaterally close Pennsylvania Avenue forever, even though it was never clear whether the initial closure in 1995 had been intended to be temporary or permanent.

Thus, this study was undertaken to emphasize that any decision about the fate of Pennsylvania Avenue should be attended by the broad consultation and independent assessment that attended the initial decision to close it—that is, that the issue deserved, and indeed required, a broader solicitation of views. In fact, this democratic process was fulfilled in the series of NCPC hearings that began in March 2001 and culminated in the recommendations detailed in the NCPC report.

The RAND staff who worked on this study contributed directly to those hearings, and we believe that our assessment, with its emphasis on the need for a more democratic process that entertains the views of all key stakeholders, contributed to reopening the discussions.

Acts of terrorism are not a new threat to Washington, D.C. Over the past two centuries, several organized terrorist attacks and numerous assaults by unstable individuals acting alone have targeted the White House, the U.S. Capitol building, the President, or U.S. congressmen within the city limits of the District of Columbia. It was not until the 1980s, however, that such incidents evoked heightened security around the White House, initiating a process of fortification that culminated in President Clinton's decision in May 1995 to close the section of Pennsylvania Avenue directly in front of the Executive Mansion.

The study presented in this report assesses how Pennsylvania Avenue could be reopened without compromising the safety and security of the President. The report does not attempt to provide a detailed assessment of the physical security requirements in and around the White House or an exhaustive catalog of the possible antiterrrorism measures available to those responsible for protecting it. Rather, its purpose is to examine the context and circumstances that influenced the decision to close Pennsylvania Avenue and to assess that decision's continued validity and appropriateness in light of developments, including trends in terrorism and counterterrorism, that have occurred since 1995. The research presented here is derived exclusively from open sources: published books, newspaper and other secondary sources, public government documents, and on-the-record interviews conducted with both retired and active federal law-enforcement officials, senior appointed government officials, architects, traffic engineers, and members of local businessmen's and citizens' associations.

This work was carried out within RAND's Criminal Justice Research Program. It was sponsored by the Federal City Council[2] in support of a larger effort aimed at reassessing and reconsidering the physical security measures that have been imposed on the District of Columbia in recent years.

---

[2]The Federal City Council is a nonprofit, nonpartisan, Washington, D.C.–based organization dedicated to the improvement of the nation's capital.

CONTENTS

For most of the White House's 200-year existence, U.S. presidents embraced the Jeffersonian principle of maintaining the Executive Mansion as the "People's House"—that is, keeping it as open and accessible to the public as possible. In the 1980s, however, a series of incidents evoked heightened security around the White House, initiating a process of fortification that culminated in President Clinton's May 1995 decision to close the section of Pennsylvania Avenue in front of the Executive Mansion. This unprecedented step was taken at the behest of the U.S. Secret Service, which had concluded that it would be impossible to protect the White House from a large truck bomb if the street remained open. Five weeks earlier, a massive truck bomb had exploded outside the Alfred P. Murrah Federal Building in Oklahoma City, killing 168 persons and injuring hundreds of others. The parallels drawn between the Murrah Building blast and the potential for a similar incident at the White House were reportedly instrumental in the President's decision to accede to the Secret Service's repeated entreaties to bar all traffic from Pennsylvania Avenue between 15th and 17th Streets.

Six years later, the truncation of this vital crosstown artery, linking the western and eastern parts of the city, continues to disrupt traffic and commuting patterns, adversely affect local businesses, and hamper access to the newly revitalized downtown city center. The closure, moreover, is seen as projecting an image of fortification and security that is both undesirable and inappropriate for a nation whose defining characteristic is its open and democratic society. Perhaps most disquieting, a decision that was justified and officially explained as a response to a specific event (the Oklahoma City bombing) and that was necessarily influenced by then-existent security and technological limitations has since evolved into an established fait accompli, subject to no subsequent evaluation, discussion, or consideration.

Because the negative aspects of the closure persist, RAND was asked to examine whether it would be possible to reopen Pennsylvania Avenue and still provide the level of security needed to minimize the threat to the President from a truck bomb at the White House. This report seeks to identify the measures that could offset that threat while preserving to the greatest extent possible normal traffic patterns and daily life in the city. Its principal findings and conclusions are as follows:

1. The 1995 explosion at the Murrah Building may have less relevance than has been commonly assumed to the possibility of a similar attack directed against the White House. The vehicle containing the bomb in Oklahoma City was parked *less than ten feet away* from the structure when the blast occurred. By comparison, the White House is *set some 325 feet back from the south curb of Pennsylvania Avenue*—more than 30 times the distance between the Murrah Building and the truck containing the bomb.

2. The 1995 decision to close the section of Pennsylvania Avenue in front of the White House appears to have been regarded as permanent. Thus, in contrast to the forward-thinking, dynamic responses that characterized the Clinton administration's overall approach to the terrorist threat, the issue of physical security in and around the Executive Mansion appears to have been treated in a static, one-dimensional way: The decision to close Pennsylvania Avenue has been frozen in time, and no attempt has been made to take advantage of new technologies and potentially innovative approaches to physical security developed since that time.

3. Given the increased attention, larger budgets, and greater numbers of law-enforcement and intelligence personnel devoted to strengthening U.S. counterterrorism response capabilities since the Oklahoma City bombing, the nation is arguably far better prepared to address the threat of terrorism than it has ever been. This enhanced preparedness should be as great a factor in security planning

and design as are the worst-case scenarios that now dominate security thinking.

4. Justifications for Pennsylvania Avenue's continued closure now extend beyond assuring the safety of the President and his family from truck-bomb attacks. Current White House security policy has not benefited from the independent, outside consultation and evaluation that played an important part in the 1995 decision; today's security policy is being unilaterally defined and extended by federal law-enforcement authorities.

5. The security policy for the White House is unlike that for any other federal government building or historic landmark in the District of Columbia—including the U.S. Capitol and the U.S. Supreme Court. Therefore, the extraordinary security measures in force at the Executive Mansion could, in fact, displace terrorist threats onto these other enormously symbolic, but less extensively protected—i.e., "softer"—targets.

6. A comprehensive, independent examination should be undertaken to determine whether the 800-foot setback defined by the Secret Service is in fact the absolute minimum distance required to adequately protect the Executive Mansion. This assessment should clearly explicate—and justify—the context within which setback determinations are gauged, particularly with regard to questions of acceptable and unacceptable levels of building damage.

7. Various proposed measures could secure the President's personal protection from catastrophic truck-bomb threats while still permitting open access and unrestricted freedom of movement around the nation's most important historical landmarks. Potential alternatives and options that deserve thoughtful consideration and careful evaluation include the following:

- The section of Pennsylvania Avenue between Jackson Place and Madison Place could be bounded with some form of fixed barriers constructed in a way that permits access by cars (including taxicabs) but prevents entry by trucks, buses, and unauthorized vehicles.

- Pennsylvania Avenue itself could be modified to provide greater security; for example, a modified "Jefferson bow" could be built to curve the midsection of Pennsylvania Avenue northward, adding another 60 feet of standoff distance in front of the White House.

- Physical countermeasures could be enhanced through the introduction of state-of-the-art detection technology, including video surveillance and explosive-trace sensors. Such innovations could be combined with a reconfigured executive protection force that would provide additional deterrent value.

Such proposals should not be blindly dismissed for the sake of maintaining complete control over the presently closed section of Pennsylvania Avenue or to preserve the status quo because any alternative is assumed to be either too risky or too complicated. Indeed, none of these measures is foolproof, and all could conceivably be defeated by a determined suicide attack involving a fanatical terrorist. The same caveat, of course, applies to the entire spectrum of threats directed against the President. The issue here is not protection of the President from *all possible* contingencies; it is the enacting of appropriate security measures that address reasonable threat contingencies within the context of an acceptable level of risk.

The Executive Mansion's defensive arrangements must reflect the openness and vitality that are defining characteristics of the United States and also project an image of strength and confidence consonant with being the leader of the free world, the lone superpower. The security surrounding the White House is thus a critical element of the building's symbolic function. By imposing unnecessarily disruptive antiterrorist measures, the United States risks presenting an undesirable and unwanted image. Accordingly, the fundamental challenge is that of achieving an equitable balance between these competing requirements and at the same time minimizing public disruption and inconvenience.

ACKNOWLEDGMENTS

The authors wish to thank RAND colleagues Melissa Bradley and Barbara Williams for their assistance and advice in the preparation of this report. They are also grateful to Brian Michael Jenkins, one of the world's foremost authorities on terrorism and security issues, whose detailed technical review of an earlier draft of this document greatly enhanced the final product. Several persons who were either involved in or had particular knowledge of the deliberations that led to the 1995 closure of the portion of Pennsylvania Avenue immediately in front of the White House were immensely helpful, assisting the authors in understanding the context of and the circumstances surrounding that decision. Similarly, the U.S. Secret Service and the staff at the Washington Field Office of the Federal Bureau of Investigation were generous with their time, sharing their expertise with the RAND project staff and greatly facilitating a useful exchange of views. Finally, the authors are particularly indebted to Janet DeLand, whose incomparably deft and finely honed editorial skills significantly improved the clarity and presentation of this report. Her assistance and that of RAND's Publications Department are greatly appreciated.

Chapter One

INTRODUCTION

When President Clinton left office in January 2001, he could claim credit for having done more than any other president to ensure that America is prepared to counter terrorist threats. During his two administrations, overall spending on countering and defending against terrorism doubled. The budgets of key individual agencies charged with this mission increased exponentially, and three seminal Presidential Decision Directives redefined departmental responsibilities and provided greater coordination of governmental efforts. Most critically, terrorism was elevated to the very top of the list of security threats that the United States will have to face in the 21st century.

Another legacy of the Clinton administration's ambitious counterterrorist efforts, however, is the more controversial presidential decision to close the portion of Pennsylvania Avenue immediately in front of the White House.[1] This unprecedented action, implemented in May 1995, was taken at the behest of the U.S. Secret Service, which had concluded that it would be impossible to protect the White House from a large truck bomb as long as traffic was allowed to travel on Pennsylvania Avenue between 15th and 17th Streets. Only five weeks earlier, a massive truck bomb had exploded outside the Alfred P. Murrah Federal Building in Oklahoma City, killing 168 persons and injuring hundreds of others. The parallels drawn between the Murrah Building blast and the potential for a similar incident in front

---

[1] In addition to the closure of this section of Pennsylvania Avenue to the north of the White House, all westbound traffic on E Street, to the south, around the Ellipse, was also prohibited.

of the White House were reportedly instrumental in the President's decision to finally accede to the Secret Service's repeated entreaties.[2]

Six years later, the truncation of this vital crosstown artery, linking the western and eastern parts of the city, continues to disrupt traffic and commuting patterns,[3] to adversely affect local businesses, and to hamper access to the newly revitalized downtown city center.[4] In addition to the inconvenience[5] and revenue loss[6] it has created, the closure is seen as projecting an image of fortification and security that is both undesirable and inappropriate for a nation whose defin-

_____

[2]Information obtained in interviews and discussions held in May and June 2000 with federal law-enforcement officials involved in the 1994–1995 reviews of White House security and with members of the commission convened to advise the U.S. Treasury Department on this issue.

[3]Altered traffic patterns resulting from the closure of Pennsylvania Avenue have displaced a significant number of vehicles onto contiguous streets, creating severe congestion problems in the downtown area. Between 27,000 and 28,000 cars a day traveled along Pennsylvania Avenue between 15th and 17th Streets prior to May 1995; most of this traffic is now forced to use Constitution Avenue and H, I, and K Streets. Traffic volumes on these routes have since risen by between 30 and 50 percent, which has severely impacted the east-west flow of traffic in the District. H and I are relatively narrow, and their conversion to one-way streets in 1995 did less to ameliorate traffic congestion than had been either anticipated or hoped for by at least some members of the advisory commission (discussions with Parsons Transportation, Washington, D.C., May 24, 2000; William T. Coleman, Washington, D.C., June 2, 2000; and William H. Webster, Washington, D.C., June 8, 2000).

[4]Closing Pennsylvania Avenue has hampered business efficiency in the downtown area by increasing traffic volume and congestion at key intersections. For certain firms this has meant higher overhead costs (e.g., higher delivery and consignment charges), while for others it has led to a decline in productivity because of longer employee commuting times. It has compromised two principal reasons for con- ducting business in the District: proximity and convenience. Several firms have chosen to relocate from the inner downtown area, lowering retail sales and property values and in turn decreasing the District's overall revenue base.

[5]Anecdotal evidence from office workers, shoppers, commuters, and cabdrivers suggests that the trip across downtown has increased by at least 15 minutes and, depending on the time of day, possibly by as much as 45 minutes (Fehr, 1997).

[6]Direct losses resulting from reduced parking meter and ticket revenue plus higher Metrobus capital expenses resulting from the forced rerouting of scheduled services have been estimated at $460,628 a year. Since 1995, parking meter losses alone have amounted to more than $728,000, and modifications to the Washington Metropolitan Area Transit Authority (WMTA) network have cost the District an additional $1,575,000. (See Labaton, 1995.)

ing characteristic is its open and democratic society.[7] Perhaps most disquieting, a decision that was justified and officially explained as a response to a specific event (the Oklahoma City bombing) and that was necessarily influenced by then-existent security and technological limitations has since evolved into an established fait accompli, subject to no subsequent evaluation, discussion, or consideration. In retrospect, another unfortunate consequence of the 1995 decision was that no formal process was either identified or established that could take into account any additional protective measures, strengthened counterterrorist policies, new security approaches, or improved technologies—developments that could be of considerable relevance today in defending against the threat posed by a truck bomb to the White House. Given the forward-thinking, dynamic responses to the terrorist threat that characterized the Clinton administration's overall antiterrorism approach, it is somewhat bewildering that the same dynamism and innovation have not been applied to the basic security decisions directly affecting the White House. On the contrary, physical security in and around the Executive Mansion appears to have been treated in a static, one-dimensional way: The decision to close Pennsylvania Avenue has been frozen in time; moreover, it addresses only one subset of threats to the President (bomb attacks, and more specifically, truck bombs).

ORGANIZATION AND METHODOLOGY OF THIS STUDY

RAND was asked to assess whether it would be possible to reopen Pennsylvania Avenue and still provide the level of security needed to minimize the threat to the President from a truck bomb at the White House. This report seeks to identify measures that could offset that threat while preserving to the greatest extent possible normal traffic patterns and daily life in the city. No attempt has been made to provide a detailed assessment of the physical security requirements in and around the White House or an exhaustive catalog of possible antiterrrorism measures available to those responsible for protecting

---

[7]See Moynihan, 1999; U.S. General Services Administration and U.S. Department of State, in cooperation with the American Institute of Architects, 2000, passim; and Forgey, 1999.

it. Rather, by examining the context and circumstances that influenced the 1995 decision to close Pennsylvania Avenue, this study raises pertinent questions regarding the validity and appropriateness of that decision today in light of developments over the past six years, including trends in terrorism and counterterrorism.

The research approach was conceived both to illuminate the disruption, inconvenience, and adverse effects of the closure of Pennsylvania Avenue and to better appreciate the broad challenges faced by federal law-enforcement agencies responsible for defending Washington, D.C., against terrorist attack—in particular, the U.S. Secret Service, which is charged with protecting the President and his family. Five key questions guided this research:

1. What were the primary factors involved in the decision to close a section of Pennsylvania Avenue to vehicular traffic in 1995?

2. After the decision to close Pennsylvania Avenue was made, was any thought given to assessing how long it should stay closed (e.g., was the decision regarded as a *permanent* solution)?

3. Have any alternatives to the closure of Pennsylvania Avenue been examined recently?

4. Have the responses of other major capital cities faced with sustained terrorist threats and serious incidents of violence been examined?

5. What is perceived to be the most serious threat to Washington, D.C., posed by terrorists today?

To address the fourth question above, we examined the experiences of London and Paris, seeking applicable lessons, technologies, and approaches to providing security and countering terrorism that might be relevant to the District of Columbia.

The methodology included a detailed literature search and in-depth interviews with former and current federal law-enforcement officials who have particular knowledge and experience concerning security issues in the Washington, D.C., area; members of the commission convened by the Treasury Department in 1994–1995 to assess White House security; and other informed persons. The survey instrument designed for the project is reproduced in Appendix A.

Two caveats should be noted: First, at the risk of stating the obvious, the issue of security and protection against terrorist attack in the nation's capital in general and the White House in particular is a highly sensitive, emotionally charged subject. While some federal law-enforcement agencies were forthcoming and frank in their depictions and explanations of the problem, other key federal agencies were initially reluctant to discuss these issues with the project research staff. Only after an early draft of this report was widely noted in the press[8] did representatives of those agencies directly responsible for presidential and White House security agree to meet with us and exchange views. The security personnel of some foreign embassies in Washington also declined to discuss the policies and procedures in force around the official residences and important landmarks in their own nations' capitals for fear of compromising otherwise good relations with their American counterparts.

Second, as Brian Jenkins, one of the world's leading experts on terrorism and security, has cogently argued, security is never simply a matter of assessing the threat and then deciding with complete confidence on a set of incontestably appropriate and effective protective measures. A range of factors, including many that are not quantifiable and have no clear metrics of either success or effectiveness, necessarily enter into such calculations. It is necessary to consider potential loss of life and the possibility of widespread injuries; economic damage; adverse political consequences; increased security costs and requirements for architectural adjustments; public attitudes toward disruption and changes; public reactions to increased inconvenience; effects on citizens' individual sense of freedom and liberty; political image; ease of circumvention of the protective measures; displacement of risk onto other targets; aesthetics; and many other factors. Tradeoffs are not only involved but inevitable in the design of security measures and the decisionmaking process that leads to their implementation. As Jenkins noted with specific reference to the issue of presidential security, "The consequences of an attack overwhelm any estimate of its probability."[9] The issues of tradeoffs and the weighing of consequences versus probability (no

---

[8]See, for example, Forgey, 2000a,b; Clymer, 2000; Fehr, 2000; and Editorial, *The Washington Post*, September 28, 2000.

[9]Jenkins, 1991, p. 91.

matter how debated) are critical to the determination of appropriate security levels around any potential terrorist target. We make no claim of any particular prescience regarding the security of the President and the Executive Mansion. At the same time, however, we believe strongly in the importance and the propriety of asking pertinent questions—even at the risk of raising highly sensitive security issues—to prompt further official explication and to stimulate public debate and discussion.

Chapter Two of this report provides a historical overview of security in and around the White House and examines the events leading up to the 1995 decision to close Pennsylvania Avenue. It also considers that decision within the context of contemporary terrorism trends, both domestic and international, and how they have affected perceptions of threat and vulnerability. Chapter Three examines the principal issues involved in the challenge of countering terrorism and identifies relevant law-enforcement and security concerns. It assesses these concerns within the context of potentially promising alternatives to the continued closure of Pennsylvania Avenue that have emerged since 1995. Chapter Four focuses on the security measures in force around landmarks and the residences of heads of state in some foreign capital cities and considers their relevance to security in the United States. Finally, Chapter Five presents our findings and recommendations.

Chapter Two

THE DECISION TO CLOSE PENNSYLVANIA AVENUE: A HISTORICAL OVERVIEW OF SECURITY AT THE WHITE HOUSE FROM 1800 TO 2000

Acts of terrorism are not a new threat to Washington, D.C. Over the past two centuries, several organized terrorist attacks and numerous attacks by unstable individuals acting alone have targeted either the President of the United States or U.S. congressmen within the city limits of the District of Columbia. However, it was not until the 1980s that such attacks led federal law-enforcement agencies to heighten security around the White House and the U.S. Capitol. Three specific incidents involving the Executive Mansion occurred in 1994, and the following year the decision was made to close Pennsylvania Avenue. Ironically, even this extreme security measure would have done little to either prevent or deter the three 1994 incidents or any subsequent attacks. In fact, terrorist attacks *outside* the Washington, D.C., metropolitan area—and outside the United States as well—have been the dominant influence on the security measures in force in and around the White House today.

This chapter examines the physical security measures that have been implemented to protect the White House complex throughout its 200-year existence, with a particular focus on measures that have been imposed in recent years because of heightened fears and concerns about terrorism.

THE FIRST 183 YEARS

For most of the White House's 200-year existence,[1] U.S. presidents embraced the Jeffersonian principle of maintaining the Executive Mansion as the "People's House"—that is, keeping it as open and accessible to the public as possible. Indeed, until the first part of the 20th century, presidents and their wives would regularly greet visitors briefly during the lunch hour. President Jefferson himself granted almost unfettered access to the White House, imposing restrictions only early in the morning, while he was asleep, or when he was out of town. Although three presidents fell victim to assassins during the 19th century—Lincoln (1865), Garfield (1881), and Harrison (1885)— two of them (Lincoln and Garfield) in Washington, D.C., access to the White House was not curtailed until the Spanish-American War.

The public enjoyed even freer rein on the White House grounds. The White House gardens provided an unobstructed view of the Potomac River and were a prime tourist attraction in the early part of the 19th century. Admission to the grounds was regulated only by a series of walls and fences constructed over a period of time beginning in Jefferson's tenure. Eventually, guards were employed to manage the flow of visitors to the grounds, but the public was admitted freely during daylight hours until World War II.

Although the public had considerable access to the White House and its grounds, this does not imply that there was a complete lack of security within and around the White House complex. President Jefferson ordered the construction of a high stone wall to replace the temporary rail-fence that once surrounded the White House grounds. But because a portion of the northern wall blocked the view of the Executive Mansion from present-day Lafayette Park, President Monroe replaced the wall with a curving iron fence. An iron fence was also constructed on the west and east sides of the White House, and gates with heavy locks were installed.

---

[1]Building of the original White House commenced in 1792. That building was first occupied by President and Mrs. John Adams in 1800. The present structure was built in 1818, following the destruction of the original White House four years earlier by British troops during the War of 1812.

Until 1835, the iron fence was the most visible and only physical security structure at the White House. This changed in January 1835, when a man identified as Richard Lawrence fired two pistols at President Andrew Jackson during funeral services for Representative Warren R. Davis in the House chamber of the U.S. Capitol. Jackson was not harmed, as both pistols misfired. Nonetheless, a wooden "watch box" for a sentry was installed on the south grounds at the gate to the President's garden.[2]

Until early in the 20th century, security for the President consisted mainly of guards in civilian dress, recruited from the marshal of the District of Columbia. During special events and when the public was invited to the White House, the number of guards would be increased. In addition to the guards, a doorkeeper was assigned to maintain watch in the entrance hall. Although he was not armed, the doorkeeper always had firearms close at hand. Not all presidents approved of the guard system. John Adams, John Quincy Adams, and Andrew Jackson were against it. Holding the opposite view, James Monroe required it. However, it was not until 1842, during the Tyler administration, that a permanent company of guards was established to protect the President and the White House complex. Two events prompted this action: In 1841, an intoxicated individual entered the White House grounds and threw stones at President Tyler as he walked along the south side of the complex. (This was probably the closest a president has come to being physically harmed on White House grounds.) Then, in 1842 an enraged and intoxicated Whig mob, protesting President Tyler's veto of a bill to create the Second Bank of the United States, gathered outside the White House's locked gates, throwing stones, firing guns, and burning the President in effigy.

Physical security measures, however, remained largely unchanged until World War II, except in times of war. During the Civil War, troops took up positions in the mansion until the District of Columbia was determined to be sufficiently fortified, but no additional physical barriers were constructed. In 1942, after the United States had officially entered World War II, guardhouses manned by a special detachment of Military Police were placed at regular intervals

---

[2]U.S. Department of the Treasury, 1995c.

both inside and outside the fence. Also, armed sentries stood around-the-clock watch on the White House roof until near the end of the war, when they were assigned elsewhere.

The physical security measures that remained in place after World War II were designed primarily to prevent forcible intrusions by lone individuals or assassins. Even the November 1950 attempt on the life of President Truman at Blair House by Puerto Rican nationalists did not result in increased physical security measures at the White House. It was reasoned that having President Truman reside in Blair House while renovations were being completed at the White House had amplified the security risk, since the architectural design and the placement of Blair House made it a limited-security environment. The building was separated from the sidewalk by five feet of front lawn, a shoulder-high wrought-iron fence, and a low hedge, whereas the White House had more than 60 yards of front lawn, a 12-foot-high fence, and numerous sentry posts.[3] The actual physical threat to the President, therefore, was deemed to have receded when he and his family moved back into the White House.

Whereas several violent incidents have occurred on the perimeter of the White House grounds over the past 150 years, attempts to forcibly enter the White House complex have become more frequent and more violent in the past 50 years—and particularly the last 26 years. These intrusions have come from both the ground and the air, and some have prompted increased physical security measures. In February 1974, Private Robert Preston, a U.S. Army helicopter mechanic, stole a military helicopter from Fort Meade, Maryland, and flew it over the Executive Mansion. He then hovered over the south lawn and touched down briefly approximately 150 feet from the west wing before flying away. Preston returned a short time later and was forced by the Executive Protection Agency to land, in a hail of shotgun and submachine-gun fire.[4]

On Christmas Day of the same year, a man dressed in Arab clothing, claiming to be the Messiah and to be laden with explosives, crashed his car through the northwest gate of the White House complex and

---

[3]Smith, 1998.

[4]*The New York Times*, February 17, 1974, pp. 1 and 6.

drove up to the north portico, several feet from the front door. Following a four-hour standoff, the intruder, whose name was Marshall Fields, surrendered. The "explosives" strapped to his body turned out to be harmless flares.[5] In both of the above instances, the President and his family were not at home.

The Secret Service conducted a security review following these two events, despite spokesman George Cosper's comment that White House security measures were adequate, and in 1976, the 19th century wrought-iron gates were replaced with stronger, reinforced gates. The same year, Stephen B. Williams attempted unsuccessfully to ram his pickup truck through the new northwest gate. Unlike the truck, the gate did not buckle.

Although these attempts to penetrate the White House grounds were indeed violent and may have had the deliberate intention of harming the President, none was considered indicative of a trend to carry out large-scale attacks to destroy or severely damage the White House complex; nor did trends in international or domestic terrorism at the time support such concerns.[6] Accordingly, closing off Pennsylvania Avenue to prevent terrorist attacks was not seriously considered until the early 1980s. The only previous documented discussions of closing Pennsylvania Avenue occurred during President Kennedy's tenure in office, and at that time, the motivation for closure was purely aesthetic. During the Kennedy administration, architects working on a project to preserve buildings along Lafayette Square offered the President and the First Lady the option of turning the avenue in front of the White House into a pedestrian plaza with fountains on each end, raised flower beds in the middle, and light gray granite as the surface.[7] But the proposal foundered following President Kennedy's assassination in November 1963.[8]

Until 1983, the security measures in place at the White House reflected the types of threats considered most likely to be encountered

---

[5] *The New York Times*, December 26, 1974, p. 1.

[6] For an assessment of trends in international and domestic terrorism at that time, see Hoffman, 1993.

[7] Brown and Torry, 1995, p. A1.

[8] Warnecke, 1998, p. C2.

there. Since that time, however, a series of incidents both at the White House and outside the District of Columbia has resulted in the implementation of increasingly strict security measures to protect the physical structures of the White House complex. These incidents have varied from international terrorist attacks on American targets overseas to direct attacks on the White House and other federal and nongovernment buildings within the United States. Most of the incidents were individual acts of violence, apparently not tied to larger terrorist movements.

In 1983, after a series of suicide car and truck bombings of American targets in the Middle East by Islamic terrorists, the explosion of a small bomb outside the Senate chamber in the U.S. Capitol building, and intelligence reports that pro-Iranian terrorists were planning to attack major U.S. installations, the Secret Service began to implement an antiterrorist plan that called for increased security at the White House complex, including some permanent alterations to the White House grounds. During the 1983 Thanksgiving holiday, the Secret Service reacted to intelligence reports that pro-Iranian Shiite Muslims were planning a major attack against a U.S. installation by placing trucks filled with sand at most of the gates to the White House complex, as well as at the State Department.[9] Three trucks were parked at the southwest gate, another was parked inside the northwest gate, and two more were parked inside gates off 17th Street, leading to the Old Executive Building. A seventh truck was placed on the east side of the White House, next to the Treasury Building. Within two weeks, the Secret Service replaced three of the trucks with sand-filled concrete walls known as Jersey Barriers. The barriers were installed at the intersection of State Place and West Executive Avenue, an entrance frequently used by foreign visitors, guests, and other dignitaries. A similar, small concrete barrier was erected at a park across from the south side of the White House.[10] As an additional precaution against truck bombs, iron bars were installed that rise out of the ground when the gates are shut.[11] The original plans did not call for barriers at the gates on Pennsylvania

---

[9]"White House Security Explained," 1983, p. A21.

[10]Schribman, 1983, p. A31.

[11]Gailey, 1983, pp. A1 and 24.

Avenue; however, the following year, masonry piers were installed along the curb in front of the White House.[12]

The 1983 truck bombing of the U.S. Marine barracks in Beirut and the 1981 assassination attempt on President Reagan prompted the Secret Service to explore the option of closing Pennsylvania Avenue. The Reagan administration asked Carl Warnecke, a well-known District of Columbia architect, to design plans for alternative uses of Pennsylvania Avenue. As he had proposed 20 years earlier to President and Mrs. Kennedy, Warnecke suggested the creation of a pedestrian plaza in front of the White House and the construction of a tunnel under Pennsylvania Avenue for vehicular traffic.[13] Like its predecessor, this scheme also languished.

In early 1984, the White House implemented tightened security plans that had been under review for almost a year. The increased security was spurred not only by the aforementioned terrorist bombings in the Middle East, but also by the shooting of an armed man outside the White House by a Secret Service agent. Accordingly, since 1984, guards with bomb-sniffing dogs have checked each car entering the White House complex. Media and visitor access to the Executive Mansion is now restricted to two gates at which those entering are checked with magnetometers for concealed weapons. Previously, persons entering the White House had been required only to present their credentials or visitors' permits.[14]

From the 1980s, when the Reagan administration implemented its antiterrorist security measures to fortify White House security, until the mid-1990s, only slight modifications were made to overall White House complex security. Additional concrete barriers and masonry piers were placed around the entire complex, advanced electronic sensors were installed around the perimeter, and surveillance from the White House rooftop was increased. But until the mid-1990s, no further modifications were deemed necessary. The measures in

---

[12]Ibid., p. 31; Fehr, 1995a, p. A1.

[13]Brown and Torry, 1995.

[14]Reuters, 1984, p. A12.

place were considered sufficient to ensure both the safety of the President and the security of the Executive Mansion.[15]

1994 TO THE PRESENT

Even before the Oklahoma City bombing, which prompted the most significant changes in security policy at the White House and its environs in the nation's history, the Secret Service reportedly had wanted to close Pennsylvania Avenue. Three unrelated incidents in the fall and winter of 1994 provided the initial arguments in favor of such closure.[16] The first incident occurred in September: A 38-year-old man with a history of alcohol and substance abuse stole a small private aircraft from an airport in Maryland and intentionally crashed it into the White House. Although no one was harmed or killed (except the man himself, who died in the crash, thought to have been a deliberate act of suicide), the incident highlighted the building's vulnerability to a determined—and suicidal—adversary. The following month, a lone gunman opened fire on the White House with a semiautomatic assault rifle. He fired some 29 rounds into the north façade of the building, one of which penetrated a window in the press briefing room in the west wing. In the third incident, in December, the mansion was struck by bullets fired from somewhere south of the White House grounds.[17]

Although none of the attacks appears to have been politically motivated—thus none can be considered an act of terrorism per se[18]— and they did not cause any serious harm or damage to either individuals or the building itself, the three incidents fed a climate of fear and concern over terrorism that had been growing in the United States since the previous year's bombing of the World Trade Center in New York City. That attack, which occurred within weeks of President Clinton's inauguration, sent shock waves throughout the coun-

---

[15]Fehr, 1995a.

[16]Discussions with Judge William H. Webster (June 8, 2000); William T. Coleman, a former Secretary of Transportation (June 2, 2000); and Gary Burch, former Chief Engineer for the District of Columbia, and Harvey Joyner, both of Parsons Transportation (May 24, 2000).

[17]Additional details of these incidents are given in Appendix B.

[18]Terrorism is defined here as a politically motivated act of violence.

try. A bomb weighing approximately 1,200 pounds, constructed from readily available commercial ingredients (urea and nitric acid) with its explosive power further enhanced by three metal cylinders of compressed hydrogen gas,[19] killed six persons and injured more than a thousand others. The casualty toll would have been far greater had the terrorists who detonated the bomb succeeded in their intention of toppling one of the twin towers onto the other.

The significance of the 1993 World Trade Center blast and its impact on the American psyche cannot be overstated. Until then, terrorism had been widely perceived by Americans as something that happened elsewhere. No matter how frequently U.S. citizens and interests were the targets of terrorists abroad, many Americans believed that the United States itself was somehow immune to such violence within its own borders. The Trade Center bombing shattered that complacency and raised concerns about the security of potential targets across the United States—and in Washington, D.C., in particular—as no previous terrorist incident had done. Indeed, despite a history of attacks on American presidents within the United States—one in four has been the target of an assassination attempt[20]—it was only in the aftermath of the World Trade Center bombing and the three 1994 incidents at the White House that the extraordinary security measures now in effect around the White House began to take shape.

A commission was established to review the security needs at the White House complex and advise the Treasury Department on a variety of issues—including whether Pennsylvania Avenue between 15th and 17th Streets should be closed. The commission, which consisted primarily of experts from outside the government, was directed by former Treasury Secretary Lloyd Bentsen[21] to examine and evaluate all the facts surrounding the September 1994 aircraft crash; the security procedures then in force in and around the White House

---

[19]Reeve, 1999, pp. 6, 7, and 154.

[20]According to Franklin L. Ford (1985, p. 355), nine presidents have been the targets of assassination attempts (one of them twice), as have one president-elect and three presidential candidates.

[21]Under Secretary of the Treasury for Enforcement Ronald K. Noble and Secret Service Director Eljay B. Bowman also appear to have been key Treasury Department players on the commission.

complex; the complex's vulnerability to air and ground attacks; and the utilization of state-of-the-art technologies to enhance protection from such attacks. It was also charged with finding a way to address the "need to keep the White House as open and accessible to the public as possible consistent with valid security needs"—specifically in relation to restricting vehicular access to Pennsylvania Avenue.[22]

After eight months of study, the commission recommended that the section of Pennsylvania Avenue directly in front of the White House be closed to all vehicular traffic and made into a pedestrian zone, on the grounds that the President and the Executive Mansion could not otherwise be protected from a large truck-bomb explosion.[23] The recommendation of the panel, after consultations with White House staff, was approved by Treasury Secretary Robert Rubin and was eventually put into effect on May 19, 1995.[24] The initial step toward closure of the avenue was the placement of barriers on the northwest and northeast intersections of Pennsylvania Avenue and 15th and 17th Streets. These barriers were eventually replaced with guard-houses, automatic underground metal barriers that could be raised and lowered, and large concrete planters.

Initially, the White House rejected the commission's findings, fearing that they would send an undesirable symbolic message of sealing off government and separating the President from the people. This assessment changed, however, following the Oklahoma City bombing. But in fact, that attack had less relevance to the threat of a truck-bomb attack on the White House than is commonly assumed. In the first place, the vehicle containing the estimated 4,800- to 5,000-pound bomb that destroyed the Murrah Building had been parked in an indented passenger loading zone *less than ten feet* from the center of the north side of the building. By comparison, the White House is set *some 325 feet back* from the south curb of Pennsylvania

---

[22]U.S. Department of the Treasury, 1995.

[23]See the statement of Assistant Treasury Secretary for Enforcement Jim Johnson quoted in Fehr and Reid (1996). See also Lewis, 1997; Goshko and Bowles, 1995, p. A1; Fehr and Harris, 1995a, p. A1; and Fehr and Harris, 1995b, p. B3.

[24]U.S. Department of the Treasury, 1995.

Avenue—more than 30 times the distance between the Murrah Building and the truck bomb. Second, apparently by sheer chance, the explosion occurred very close to one of the Murrah Building's four main support columns. The explosive force initiated a chain reaction, toppling each of the two-story columns in succession, collapsing the entire north façade of the building, and causing each of its nine floors to crash downward onto the one below.[25] The White House, in contrast, is built on only three levels and has a low-set, "box-type" geometrical configuration built around a framed steel structure. These structural characteristics not only minimize the danger of successive floor collapse but also help ensure that any explosive damage to the building will be localized and not catastrophic.[26]

Despite the fundamental differences between the Murrah Building blast and any potentially similar attack on the front of the White House, the incident apparently refocused President Clinton's attention on the Secret Service's assessment that the only way to protect the White House from such an attack was to eliminate all vehicular traffic from the street facing it.[27] There is no way of knowing whether President Clinton would have ultimately acceded to the recommendation to close Pennsylvania Avenue if the Oklahoma City bombing had not occurred; it was an option that he had previously consistently rejected. In any case, effective Saturday morning, May 20, 1995, Pennsylvania Avenue was closed to all vehicular traffic between 15th and 17th Streets.[28]

---

[25]Moore, 2000, p. 168. See also "Explosion in Oklahoma City," 1995.

[26]See National Research Council, 1985, p. 56; Elliot, 1986, p. 505; and Lewis, 1997, p. F1.

[27]Labaton, 1995.

[28]U.S. Department of the Treasury, 1995b. The decision was communicated to the government of the District of Columbia only the previous evening. Moreover, it was also decided that all westbound traffic on E Street and Madison Place to the east of Layfayette Park should be eliminated (discussion with a former senior Federal Bureau of Investigation [FBI] official responsible for counterterrorism, May 30, 2000). Similar views were also expressed by current FBI officials. (See also Fehr and Reid, 1996; and Jackson-Han, 1995.)

Chapter Three

SECURITY OPTIONS AND ALTERNATIVES TO CONTINUED CLOSURE OF PENNSYLVANIA AVENUE

The 1995 decision to close a portion of Pennsylvania Avenue appears to have been regarded as permanent. No consideration seems to have been given to establishing a process by which the decision could subsequently be reviewed and reassessed in light of new developments—changing trends in terrorism or the advent of new technologies and sophisticated countermeasures—or reevaluated on any regularly established, periodic basis.[1] In retrospect, this appears to have been one of the main drawbacks of the decisionmaking process at the time; arguments now used to justify the decision go well beyond earlier public statements suggesting that the closure was implemented solely to assure the safety of the President and his family from cataclysmic truck-bomb attacks.

Moreover, in the six years since the decision was made, federal law-enforcement authorities appear to have progressively "moved the goal posts" from the specific priority of executive protection to the broader goal of ensuring that the decision will not be revisited.[2] This action, which does not appear to have involved any independent, outside consultation, has unilaterally created an almost "sacred precinct" of security around the White House unlike that at any other federal government building or historic landmark—even the U.S.

---

[1]Interviews and discussions carried out by the project research staff during May, June, and October 2000.

[2]Discussions with federal officials and a former member of the Pennsylvania Avenue Task Force, Washington, D.C., June 27, 2000.

Capitol and the U.S. Supreme Court.[3] Protection of the White House façade from even minimal or cosmetic damage has become as much a factor in Pennsylvania Avenue's continued closure as is the safety of the President and his family. This chapter revisits the rationale behind the original decision and considers the arguments for continued closure. It then examines a possible alternative security architecture embracing a variety of specific options that could prove as effective as the current policy while offering added protective measures that may not have existed six years ago.

THE ARGUMENTS FOR CONTINUED CLOSURE

Federal law-enforcement officials with whom we spoke strongly oppose the reopening of Pennsylvania Avenue.[4] To their minds, it is neither necessary nor judicious to even consider reopening the street in front of the White House to traffic. Their attitude, in general, is that most people who live and work in the District have become inured to the closure, seeing congestion in the downtown area as just one more inconvenience in a city that is already beset by myriad intractable traffic problems. Moreover, they argue that people in the the nation's capital are far more security-conscious and sensitive than people in any other major American metropolis, and that they generally accept the closure of important streets and the creation of obtrusive physical security measures as entirely reasonable and necessary. Finally, the officials point out that because of the inherently transient nature of employment for many government workers— either political appointees or individuals serving a designated tour of duty with a governmental agency or at a military base in the District—a large number of these people have never known Pennsylvania Avenue as anything but closed. Therefore, for this portion of the population, reopening the street is, in the minds of federal law-enforcement officials, essentially a "non-issue."[5]

---

[3]Ibid.

[4]Interviews and discussions with retired and currently serving FBI agents responsible for counterterrorism at the national level or in Washington, D.C., May and June 2000, and with senior U.S. Secret Service and Department of the Treasury officials, October 2000.

[5]Discussion with FBI officials, Washington Field Office, Washington, D.C., May 30, 2000.

These officials also reject claims concerning the negative economic impact of closing Pennsylvania Avenue. They argue that because more people are now walking rather than riding in the immediate vicinity of the White House, businesses are benefiting from an increased volume in pedestrian trade. They also deny that altered traffic patterns in front of the White House have reduced public access, arguing that the Executive Mansion remains one of the most open, frequently visited, and freely roamed executive residences in the world.

Most of their concerns, however, relate to physical security issues above and beyond the perceived impact that reopening Pennsylvania Avenue would have on the safety of the President and the security of the White House itself.[6] Three specific concerns were repeatedly emphasized:

- The structural integrity of the Executive Mansion and its ability to withstand the impact of an explosive attack.

- The detrimental effects of any attack that inflicted any visible damage whatsoever on so important a national symbol.

- The conviction that a decision to reopen Pennsylvania Avenue would be tantamount to "waving a red flag" in front of terrorists, inevitably provoking or inviting a terrorist attack.

Federal security officials vehemently dispute the claim that the White House has a high degree of natural protection against a truck bomb. They view the standard setback distance now required for American embassies, 30 meters (97.5 feet), as largely irrelevant to the White House because, they claim, the Executive Mansion is not reinforced to nearly the same degree as these more modern, often retrofitted and significantly strengthened buildings. For example, since the 1998 embassy bombings in East Africa, many American legations are now protected by extremely strong and resilient blast walls. The officials maintain that the overpressure and "shock velocity" generated

---

[6]Discussion with FBI officials, May 30, 2000, and with U.S. Secret Service and Department of the Treasury officials, October 2000.

by 1,200 to 1,800 pounds of homemade explosives,[7] a perfectly feasible payload that could be concealed in a standard truck or semi-trailer, would be sufficient to collapse the White House completely, as long as the force of the blast was appropriately channeled and directed.[8] Secret Service blast simulations and modeling have led to the requirement for a standoff distance of at least 800 feet to adequately protect the White House from this explosive force.[9] It is perhaps not coincidental that this figure equates exactly to the distance between the front of the White House and the southern curb of H Street/northern boundary of Lafayette Park and between the White House south portico and the South Street Ellipse. (However, the 800-foot setback requirement has never been publicly discussed or otherwise used to justify the 1995 closing of Pennsylvania Avenue.)

The above argument avoids consideration of whether any alternative security architecture—perhaps one involving barrier and enhanced surveillance technologies—could effectively prevent trucks or other large vehicles capable of transporting very large bombs from entering Pennsylvania Avenue and proceeding toward the front of the White House. An independent, comprehensive examination is needed to determine whether the 800-foot setback is in fact the absolute minimum distance required to adequately protect the Executive

---

[7]Homemade explosives are believed to represent a greater danger than Semtex or high-explosive (HE) compounds for several reasons, including the relative ease of component acquisition, lower cost, and the greater explosive effectiveness of the crushing/mushrooming shock wave that homemade explosives generate (as opposed to the sharp, cutting shock wave generated by commercial explosives).

[8]Discussion with a former senior FBI official responsible for counterterrorism, May 30, 2000. See also Ellis, 1999, Chap. 5.

[9]Discussion with a former senior FBI official responsible for counterterrorism, May 30, 2000. The Department of Defense has gauged the effects of a 2,000-pound blast on a framed house. Their analysis concluded that this amount of explosive would cause total destruction at a distance of 200 feet, dropping to 50 percent damage at 275 feet, and between 50 percent and no damage at 650 feet (telephone interview with e-mail follow-ups with Tom Convery, police explosives expert, Ventura County, June 6, 2000). The point is also made that structures in dense urban settings are particularly vulnerable to destruction, since the "buildings on either of the streets confine the blast wave, which increases pressure on the buildings. Because it is confined by the buildings, the pressure of the blast drops more slowly than it would if it had been let off in the open countryside" (Moore, 2000, p. 167). The White House, while not located in open countryside, is not situated on a narrow street, surrounded by the type of urban canyon that would channel and intensify the effects of such a blast.

Mansion. Such an assessment should clearly explicate—and justify—the context within which standoff determinations are made, particularly with regard to questions of acceptable and unacceptable levels of building damage. It should also address why such a "sanitized space" is required around the White House but not around any other federal building or landmark. Moreover, it must address the fact that the initial rationale for closing Pennsylvania Avenue was not to protect a sanitized space but to ensure the President's safety.

The possibility of strengthening the White House through additional structural reinforcement and retrofitting is also dismissed by many security officials. Given the sensitive nature of previous architectural and security refinements to the White House and the severe restrictions imposed on open access to such information, it is impossible to examine the veracity of that argument in an unrestricted document. The White House has reportedly been progressively "hardened" in recent years through various state-of-the-art physical security and defensive measures, including (at a minimum) installation of bullet-proof/shatter-proof glass in the windows, strengthened walls and reinforced window frames, and perhaps even bomb-blast net curtains. However, no independent verification of such reports could be obtained from published, open sources. Therefore, this study does not attempt to assess the ability of the White House to withstand various sizes and strengths of bomb blasts or the additional measures that might ensure a suitable level of protection.

The law-enforcement officers interviewed in this study rejected proposals to surround the Executive Mansion with a plexiglass shield on the grounds that the shield would not be strong enough to withstand the effects of a major explosive force and would itself become a dangerous antipersonnel weapon when shards of sharpened plastic turned into deadly pieces of shrapnel. More formidable (but probably nontransparent) blast barriers of the sort employed outside U.S. embassies could be used, but to ensure that explosive shock waves would "roll" over the White House, they would have to be so high that they would obscure the building and completely negate the White House's symbolic function and purpose.

Some law-enforcement officers also pointed out that a shield or blast wall would compound the explosive impact of a bomb attack on the surrounding neighborhood. Contiguous buildings would be hit not only by the positive force from the primary explosion, but also by secondary shock waves deflected back from the wall. This would result in considerable loss of life among passersby or sightseers unfortunate enough to be in the vicinity of such an explosion. The shock waves would almost certainly also demolish Blair House and many other historic buildings lining Madison Place and Jackson Place, as well as the Secret Service and Park Service Police command posts on the street. The terrorists responsible for such an incident would thus enjoy the added benefit of a "picture perfect" backdrop for the inevitable television coverage.[10]

While some officials conceded that hardening of the White House's internal structure could conceivably protect the building from the most destructive effects of a major truck bomb, they emphasized that this should not be seen as an all-inclusive end in itself. Because the Executive Mansion represents the heart of American government and democracy, federal security is as concerned with preventing *any* damage to the building's façade as it is with ensuring against wholesale collapse. Preventing any physical damage whatsoever to the building has become an essential objective, one that can be achieved only by entirely eliminating the threat of a vehicular bomb in the vicinity of the White House. This apparently means maintaining the 800-foot setbacks from the front and back of the White House— which means keeping Pennsylvania Avenue permanently closed to all vehicular traffic.[11] The FBI officials maintain that Pennsylvania Avenue should be permanently converted into a pedestrian thoroughfare so that people will no longer identify the route as a roadway and thus questions about whether it should be reopened will cease to arise.[12]

Over and above questions of structural integrity of the White House, there are serious concerns that any move to relax physical security restrictions on Pennsylvania Avenue would serve as a "red flag" to terrorists, inviting—or even prompting—an attack against a reconstituted "soft target of opportunity." Relaxing physical security is simply not regarded as a viable option by law-enforcement officials,

---

[10]Discussion with FBI agents, Washington, D.C., May 30, 2000.

[11]Discussion with Parsons Corporation, Washington, D.C., May 24, 2000.

[12]Discussion with FBI agents, Washington, D.C., May 30, 2000.

especially at a time when the common perception is that the threat of terrorism is increasing.[13] The officials argue that events such as the 1996 Khobar Towers bombing in Saudi Arabia and the bombings of the American embassies in Kenya and Tanzania two years later[14] clearly demonstrate that the World Trade Center and Oklahoma City blasts were not aberrations or isolated events but were profound harbingers of heightened future violence.

However, the "red flag" argument can also be used against safety measures that are unique to the White House, since such measures could make the White House an even more attractive target for terrorists because of its aura of invincibility. The use of extraordinary and extreme measures to protect the White House is just as likely to encourage attention from terrorists as to discourage it.

Security officials are also quick to dismiss the possible utility or effectiveness of compensatory barrier control measures that might be installed at either end of Pennsylvania Avenue in front of the Executive Mansion, regarding such systems as insufficient to protect against a vehicular bomb detonated in front of the White House. The ability of automated/flexible pole systems to deter a determined suicide attack by a fanatically determined terrorist driving a large van or truck is also questioned. The officials point out that a system of this sort would require a massive crossbeam that could be impossible to deploy in time to stop a speeding vehicle.[15] However, this argument runs counter to the claims of architects and other security design specialists. At a minimum, it is an issue that requires further examination before the effectiveness of a compensatory barrier control system can be definitively determined.

Even if a sufficiently strong and maneuverable barrier could be erected, terrorists could respond by simply changing the nature of

---

[13]See, for example, National Commission on Terrorism, 2000, p. iv and passim; and the countervailing view specifically addressing that report's main argument in Bearden and Johnson, 2000.

[14]The Khobar Towers bombing killed 19 U.S. military personnel and injured more than 500 others (Americans and Saudis). The Kenya and Tanzania bombings together killed 257 people and wounded more than 5,000 others.

[15]Discussion with FBI agents, Washington, D.C., May 30, 2000. See also Ellis, 1999, p. 203.

their attack.   An enhanced ammonium-nitrate/compressed-gas-cylinder type of device launched from a car on Pennsylvania Avenue could cause considerable damage to the White House, particularly the front of the building, where at least 200 employees work. Officials have also speculated that terrorists could attempt to conceal larger bombs on tour buses that would be parked nearby, in the vicinity of Lafayette Park; the bombs could then be detonated by means of short-fuse timers. The combined overpressure and shock velocity from a delivery system of this sort could potentially be as great as that generated by a standard truck bomb.[16] However germane this argument may be, it provides further evidence that the original justification for the closing of Pennsylvania Avenue has been extended to embrace a set of security concerns far beyond the adequacy of the existing 800-foot setback.

The measured opinion of the law-enforcement and security community is thus that barrier systems can work only if they are permanently staffed by armed guards prepared to open fire against any suspect vehicle. Armed guards are, of course, already stationed in and around the White House (and other federal facilities as well) and presumably are trained and instructed to respond along precisely these lines in the event of an apparent attack.

Finally, it is argued that if Pennsylvania Avenue were reopened, every time a threat to the White House was made, the street would have to be closed down and cleared out, causing considerably more chaos and disruption than is engendered by its permanent closure. FBI agents responsible for counterterrorism in the Washington, D.C., area say that they currently receive three to four terrorist warnings a day and that temporary closures could be expected at least once every month.

However, as discussed below, a number of potentially promising options exist that might ensure security in and around the White House and protect the President while also allowing for controlled traffic flow along the currently closed section of the avenue. Some of these approaches may not have existed or may not have been apparent six years ago.

---

[16]Discussion with FBI agents, Washington Field Office, Washington, D.C., May 30, 2000.

THE ARGUMENTS AGAINST CONTINUED CLOSURE

A persuasive case can also be made against continued closure of Pennsylvania Avenue. Because the White House unquestionably deserves and requires extensive protection and security, the defensive arrangements must reflect the openness and vitality that define the United States and at the same time project an image of strength and confidence appropriate for the leader of the free world. By overreacting to the threat of terrorism and imposing unnecessarily disruptive protective measures, the United States risks presenting an undesirable and unwanted image. Accordingly, the fundamental challenge is that of achieving an equitable balance between openness and defensive strength while simultaneously minimizing public disruption and inconvenience.

Critics of the current security arrangement argue that the 1995 decision reflects a "bunker mentality" that is completely at odds with the perception of a thoroughly open society.[17] Senator Daniel Patrick Moynihan, the most eloquent exponent of this view, has stated, "We have nothing to promote if we become a fortress society. . . . The only triumph of terrorism is if we become terrified."[18] And terrifying their adversaries is of course what terrorists aim to do.

Terrorism is fundamentally the use (or threatened use) of violence to achieve profound and far-reaching psychological effects in a target audience. If the United States fails to distinguish between reasonable and catastrophic security risks, it may make choices based on fear and anxiety rather than on realistic consideration and analysis. The current focus on worst-case scenarios that dominates domestic planning and preparedness for potential acts of terrorism is a case in point. Nevertheless, the discussion following presentations at the Symposium on Security and the Design of Public Buildings in Washington, D.C., in November 2000, concluded that

> Security should be designed to meet reasonable rather than rare, catastrophic threats. A balance of risk assessment and innovative

---

[17]Comment of a participant at the Symposium on Security and the Design of Public Buildings, November 30, 1999, quoted in U.S. General Services Administration and U.S. Department of State, 2000, p. 8.

[18]Ibid., p. 1.

design can provide a high degree of security without creating a fortress. Responding to the worst-case scenario may enhance safety but at the high price of compromising a commitment to openness and accessibility.[19]

Indeed, the fixation on open-ended, low-probability threats, which in turn posit virtually limitless vulnerabilities, may not be realistic in the context of contemporary terrorist behavior and modus operandi. "This kind of analysis," Brian Jenkins warned in testimony before Congress, "can degenerate into a fact-free scaffold of anxieties and arguments—dramatic, emotionally powerful, but analytically feeble."[20]

In this respect, the law-enforcement officials protesting the reopening of Pennsylvania Avenue are ignoring the fact that the United States is almost certainly better prepared now to counter the threat of terrorism than it was six years ago. The terrorism threat and response environments should not be regarded as either static or "zero sum" in nature. Terrorist aims and motivations have changed in recent years, and terrorist capabilities have improved, as have some terrorist tactics and weapons.[21] But by the same token, such evolution and development have not occurred in a vacuum; government, law-enforcement, and intelligence capabilities have also changed and evolved. Response capabilities improve, physical security technologies advance, and new countermeasures are developed that are capable of addressing a range of potential terrorist attacks. Therefore, a comprehensive review of new security measures and technological developments in counterterrorism capabilities that have emerged since 1995 is both needed and appropriate.

Finally, the nation's worst fears of chemical and biological attacks and of massive car and truck bombings in the United States have not been realized, nor have the dire prophecies following the Tokyo nerve gas attack and the Murrah Building bombing come to pass.

---

[19]Ibid., p. 10.

[20]Jenkins, 1999, p. 4.

[21]See also the remarks of Jim Rice, Head of the Domestic Terrorism Program, National Capital Response Squad, FBI, summarized in U.S. General Services Administration and U.S. Department of State, 2000, p. 3.

This is not simply a matter of luck; it is a reflection of the fact that U.S. counterterrorist capabilities have not only improved but are continually improving. The considerable attention and resources the Clinton administration devoted to fighting terrorism appear to have thwarted persistent enemies such as Osama bin Laden since the 1998 East Africa embassy bombings—at least, until the October 2000 attack on the *U.S.S. Cole* in Aden harbor. The level of U.S. anti-terrorism preparedness should therefore be as much a factor in security planning and design as are the worst-case scenarios that are now almost reflexively embraced.

THE EFFECTS AND CONSEQUENCES
OF CONTINUED CLOSURE

The closure of Pennsylvania Avenue has physically separated the District's older central business district west of the White House from the concentration of new offices, residences, restaurants, and night-spots on the east side. The displacement of approximately 29,000 vehicles a day (the volume in 1995) from Pennsylvania Avenue onto nearby streets has created severe bottlenecks and congestion throughout the downtown area. The diverted traffic must use either H Street and I Street (a pair of one-way streets to the north), K Street, or Constitution Avenue (on the south). Traffic volume on these routes has increased by 30 to 50 percent, and the increase has severely impacted the east-west flow of traffic in the District.[22] Travel times throughout downtown Washington have increased dramatically, and the congestion has reached a level at which even the movement of emergency vehicles within and through the area has been adversely affected. Thus, the city that is meant to represent and symbolize the continuity and integration that is inherent in American society is coming to be perceived as dysfunctional.

Because the Treasury Department closed Pennsylvania Avenue with neither the advice nor the consent of Congress or of the city government and the people of the District,[23] some people view the closure as emblematic of the growing disconnection between branches of

---

[22] Discussion with Parsons Transportation, Washington, D.C., May 24, 2000.

[23]Forgey, 1999; Lewis, 1997; and Fehr and Haggerty, 1995.

the federal government and between the federal government and the city government of the District of Columbia.

As disruptive as the closing of Pennsylvania Avenue has been, many observers feel that a far more significant adverse effect has been the perception that the nation's democratic values, openness, and sense of community have been compromised. Pennsylvania Avenue is one of the principal thoroughfares in the nation's capital, and its symbolic importance is underscored by the fact that it directly connects the Legislative and Executive branches of the federal government. While most Americans recognize and accept the necessity of reasonable security precautions to protect the President and the White House, there is an equally strong sense that fundamental American values should not be sacrificed in the name of security.

POSSIBLE OPTIONS AND ALTERNATIVES TO CONTINUED CLOSURE

Pertinent questions have been raised about the actual vulnerability of the White House. As discussed above, the official, publicly stated rationale for closing Pennsylvania Avenue was the need to protect the President and the Executive Mansion from the type of cataclysmic truck bomb that destroyed the Murrah Building. However, it has been noted that the White House offers rather good natural protection from a vehicular explosive attack. A number of arguments (discussed above) have been marshaled to support this view:

- The setback area between the Executive Mansion and its northern perimeter exceeds the minimum security standard—30 meters (100 feet)—applied to U.S. embassies overseas to protect against vehicle-borne explosive attacks. The White House is set back some 325 feet from Pennsylvania Avenue, which, according to several independent analyses, is sufficient to offset the effects of a major explosive force, including even those of a large truck bomb.[24]

---

[24]See, for example, Elliot, 1986, p. 402; National Research Council, 1986, p. 31; and Strauchs, 1996.

- The White House is built on only three levels, which minimizes the danger of successive floor collapse—a critical factor in the devastation of the Murrah Building.[25]

- The White House has a low-set, "box-type" geometrical configuration built around a framed steel structure that has positive ductile qualities. These characteristics should help to ensure that any explosive damage to the mansion would be localized rather than catastrophic.[26]

Numerous design firms, structural engineers, and security contractors have stated that these features give the White House a high degree of natural resilience.[27] They have also pointed out that the building could be further strengthened and its security enhanced through additional structural reinforcement and retrofitting,[28] including

- The addition of mass and redundancy.

- The strengthening of support and street-facing walls.

- The use of galvanized shatter-proof glazing to replace the current windows.

- The incorporation of "blowout" panels and sacrificial elements to relieve and/or reduce blast pressure and amplification.[29]

A number of construction specialists have also asserted that a laminated, high-tech, explosion-resistant plexiglass fence could effectively deflect the shock wave from a truck bomb (a concept dismissed

---

[25]See National Research Council, 1985, p. 21; and Associated Press, 1995.

[26]National Research Council, 1985, p. 56; Elliot, 1986, p. 505; and Lewis, 1997.

[27]These arguments are probably based solely on information available from open, unclassified sources.

[28]Discussion with Parsons Transportation Corporation and Skidmore, Owings and Merrill (SOM) Architects, Washington, D.C., May 24 and May 30, 2000. See also Lewis, 1997.

[29]For further details of these various structural innovations see National Research Council, 1985, pp. 54–57.

by federal law-enforcement officials, as discussed above). The same idea was proposed in 1996 by the Director of the Secret Service.[30]

Finally, some private security consultants have expressed concern over the utility of closing Pennsylvania Avenue, citing the following arguments:

- Preventing vehicular traffic from traveling in front of the White House does not protect against nonexplosive threats, such as standoff, remote-controlled mortar and rocket-propelled grenade (RPG)[31] attacks; other types of assassination attempts; or airborne assaults carried out with microlight or ultralight aircraft.[32]

- Closing Pennsylvania Avenue offers a fixed and visible level of protection. One foreign security expert with executive protection experience elsewhere has suggested that less-static and more-discrete measures may be preferable for threat mitigation.[33]

- Threats to federal and government buildings elsewhere in Washington, D.C., have increased disproportionately because of the disparity between security measures at these facilities and those in and around the White House. These other historic buildings may be regarded by terrorists as "softer"—and therefore more accessible and increasingly attractive—targets.[34]

While none of these arguments in and of itself provides irrefutable justification for reassessing the 1995 decision, they *collectively* raise compelling issues that merit further consideration and discussion.

No matter what arguments are proposed in favor of reopening Pennsylvania Avenue, the most important question remains, How can this

---

[30]Discussion with Parsons Corporation, Washington, D.C., May 24, 2000. See also Moore, 1996.

[31]An RPG attack was successfully perpetrated in September 2000 against the heavily fortified headquarters of the British Secret Intelligence Service (SIS, or MI-6) in London. An RPG 22, believed to have been the weapon used, reportedly can be purchased for as little as $150 on the arms black market in Europe (Rufford, 2000).

[32]Moore, 1996; and, Lewis, 1997.

[33]Gunaratna, 2000, p. 2.

[34]Strauchs, 1996, p. 3. See also Fehr, 1995b.

be done while still providing the President, his family, and the White House staff with an appropriate level of security and also remaining true to America's long-standing commitment to openness? A number of possible security options or alternatives to closure have been proposed or are currently being examined.

One option would be to reconstruct Pennsylvania Avenue with a depressed slot configured in such a way that any blast from a truck bomb would be deflected upwards, away from the White House and surrounding buildings.[35] This alternative, however, has not received particularly favorable consideration, largely due to concerns stemming from cost, aesthetic appeal, disruption, and perceived effectiveness.[36] It is also at odds with U.S. Parks Service plans to expand underground office space and parking beneath the White House west wing, beneath Pennsylvania Avenue, and toward the New Executive Office Building across the street.[37] This proposed expansion would probably be difficult, if not impossible, to derail given the White House and Executive branch's acute need for additional office space and the attendant requirement for expanded parking facilities.

More-promising options have focused on changing the configuration of Pennsylvania Avenue itself and developing some form of barrier system that would allow access to Pennsylvania Avenue for passenger cars, including taxicabs, while preventing the entry of trucks, buses, and other large vehicles.

Prior to May 1995, Pennsylvania Avenue had three eastbound and three westbound travel lanes, plus a broad paved median strip in the area between 15th Street and 17th Street. Transportation experts who have studied the situation believe that Pennsylvania Avenue can be narrowed significantly—to two lanes in each direction—without sacrificing any of the avenue's capacity to move traffic efficiently.[38]

---

[35]Fehr, 1995a; Moore, 1996; and Warnecke, 1998, p. C2.

[36]Discussion with Parsons Transportation Corporation, Washington, D.C., May 24, 2000. Similar comments were expressed to the authors during a telephone interview with William T. Coleman, Washington, D.C., June 2, 2000.

[37]See U.S. Park Service, 1999.

[38]Discussion with Parsons Transportation Corporation, Washington, D.C., May 24, 2000.

Narrowing the roadway to a total of four lanes presupposes that these lanes would be for through traffic only and that no standing or stopping would be permitted at any time.

Narrowing the roadway would move the southern curb lane (the curb nearest the White House) an additional 40 feet to the north, moving all vehicular traffic that much farther from the White House. The setback distance from that south curb to the White House would be roughly 325 feet, more than three times the setback distance required at U.S. embassies overseas.

Urban design measures could also be applied to mitigate security concerns around the White House. Researchers investigating this possibility discovered a design recommendation for Pennsylvania Avenue that was initially suggested in 1802 by Thomas Jefferson. Jefferson proposed that the portion of Pennsylvania Avenue that extends from Madison Place to Jackson Place be gently curved to the north. This so-called "Jefferson bow" would mirror the curvilinear design of the driveway within the White House grounds. The introduction of a Jefferson bow would move the roadway an additional 60 feet from the White House, increasing the standoff distance to 385 feet.[39]

Because of the direct relationship between the size of a vehicle and the size of the explosive device it could contain, there is general agreement that it would be prudent to permanently bar large vehicles from the three-block portion of Pennsylvania Avenue in front of the White House. This would require that some form of fixed barrier be constructed that would permit access by cars while preventing entry by trucks, buses, or unauthorized vehicles.

Potentially the most effective barrier would consist of two pedestrian bridges located slightly inbound of Pennsylvania Avenue's intersections with Madison Place and Jackson Place, respectively. These bridges would have a vertical clearance of approximately 7.5 feet. The bridges would permit pedestrians to move between Lafayette Park (on the north side of the avenue) and a larger landscaped area on the north side of the White House fence (on the south side of the avenue). The pedestrian bridges, which would be structurally capa-

---

[39]Discussion with Skidmore, Owings, and Merrill, Washington, D.C., May 30, 2000.

ble of stopping any large vehicle, could be designed so that they could be removed via flatbed truck for the quadrennial Inaugural Parade. A pedestrian bridge in New York's Central Park has dimensions nearly identical to those that would be called for on Pennsylvania Avenue.[40]

In addition to new signage and pedestrian bridges that would physically preclude the entry of large vehicles to the portion of Pennsylvania Avenue in front of the White House, manned security kiosks could be located at both the 15th Street and 17th Street intersections with Pennsylvania Avenue. These manned kiosks, along with enhanced visual and electronic surveillance and the aforementioned physical changes in the configuration of Pennsylvania Avenue, would permit the controlled reopening of the avenue while providing an appropriate level of security for the President.[41]

From the standpoint of transportation usage, it would not be necessary to keep Pennsylvania Avenue open to traffic 24 hours a day. It would be possible to bar all traffic from the affected portion of the avenue from 10:00 p.m. to 6:00 a.m. without greatly impairing the movement of traffic in downtown Washington. While proponents of reopening the Avenue are not recommending this course of action, they recognize that keeping the avenue open only 16 hours a day would potentially reduce the manpower demands on the Secret Service and other law-enforcement agencies.[42] In any event, new proposals to reopen Pennsylvania Avenue have now been raised,[43] and it is up to the Department of the Treasury and the Secret Service to explicate publicly the reasons and justification for the continued retention of the present security arrangements.

---

[40]Ibid.

[41]Ibid.

[42] Discussion with Parsons Transportation Corporation, Washington, D.C., May 24, 2000.

[43]Forgey, 2000a,b; Clymer, 2000; Fehr, 2000; and Editorial, *The Washington Post,* 2000.

Chapter Four

A COMPARATIVE ASSESSMENT OF SECURITY
MEASURES IN TWO FOREIGN CAPITAL CITIES

Do security measures adopted overseas to protect against truck-bomb attacks have any relevance for the United States? Two major capitals, London and Paris, have avoided closing down major thoroughfares and avenues despite being confronted with serious campaigns of terrorism. However, in each of these cities, the measures that have been implemented reflect specific contextual circumstances and situations that clearly differ from those in the Washington, D.C., area. Nonetheless, the security arrangements in these foreign capitals are worth briefly reviewing.

LONDON

During the first half of the 1990s, London was subjected to a particularly intensive campaign of Provisional Irish Republican Army (PIRA) terrorism. Carried out under the auspices of that organization's "England Department," the most serious incidents included attacks against the Prime Minister's official residence at Number 10 Downing Street. The first attack occurred in February 1991, at the height of the Persian Gulf War, when PIRA terrorists launched several remotely controlled mortars from a van parked on Horse Guards Parade into the garden behind the executive building, shattering the windows in a room where 15 ministers and officials of the (Gulf) War Cabinet were meeting. Four people were injured in the attack.[1] The second

---

[1]Tendler, 1991; and Bennett, 1991.

incident took place a little less than a year later, in February 1992, when a PIRA incendiary device exploded less than 300 meters from Downing Street. Little damage was sustained in this attack, because the surrounding area had been evacuated following a telephone warning.[2]

Two massive truck bombings also occurred in the heart of the city's financial district—at St. Mary's Axe in 1992 and at Bishops Gate in 1993. In the St. Mary's Axe incident, described as "the most powerful explosion in London since World War II," a bomb constructed of approximately a ton of fertilizer (ammonium nitrate) exploded outside the Baltic Exchange building, killing three persons, wounding 90 others, leaving a 12-foot-wide crater, and causing $1.25 billion in damage.[3] Exactly one year later, a similar bomb in the nearby Bishops Gate district killed one person and injured more than 40 others. Initial estimates put the damage from this attack at $1.5 billion.[4] These two attacks devastated London's financial district and were intended to severely undermine London's prestige as a world financial center.[5]

The threat of future attacks and of an intensified campaign of sabotage directed against Britain's economic nerve center was taken very seriously. Accordingly, a so-called "Traffic Management Scheme" (TMS) was instituted in 1993 and has since monitored all traffic entering or leaving the square-mile inner city of London. Unofficially known as the "ring of steel," the now-routine operation involves police cordons, random vehicular checks, mobile "rolling road blocks," and high-definition closed-circuit television (CCTV) cameras positioned along critical streets and at key intersections. Every car, truck, and van that enters the city has its license plate information entered immediately into a centralized database, where it is automatically traced and cross-referenced with police and Department of Transport (DoT) national vehicular registration records. In addition, an advanced surveillance network known as Mandrake was introduced

---

[2]For further details, see Bell, 1993, p. 786; and Gearson and Freedman, 2000, pp. 10 and 12.

[3]Schmidt, 1992a,b; Schmidt, 1993; Rodgers, 1992; and Connett, 1992.

[4]Schmidt, 1993; and Stevenson, 1993.

[5]See, for instance, Milton, Burns, and Lapper, 1993.

in 1998. Mandrake is used to rapidly identify known or suspected terrorists by matching the physical facial features of pedestrians with criminal photographs stored in computerized police information banks.[6]

The implementation of this monitoring system has allowed British authorities to maintain a largely unrestricted traffic flow in the heart of London. Although Downing Street, where the Prime Minister's official residence is located, is closed to ordinary traffic, and restrictions to traffic have been introduced on the roundabout system immediately outside Buckingham Palace, closing access to the roadway around the historic fountain in front, neither street represents a major thoroughfare in terms of vehicular volume comparable to Pennsylvania Avenue. Indeed, more-important London routes such as Whitehall, Pall Mall, Victoria Embankment, and Westminster Avenue remain open, and although they pass directly in front of buildings that symbolize British power and government (the Parliament buildings and Big Ben, the Ministry of Defence, and the Foreign Ministry) or Britain's rich historical heritage (Westminster Abbey and St. Paul's Cathedral), no moves have ever been made to turn them into pedestrian walkways or to otherwise restrict vehicular traffic or access. Just as critical is the fact that, from a public management and policy viewpoint, the "ring of steel" has become an integral part of daily London life and is now largely accepted by commuters, business groups, and motoring organizations.

Introducing a scheme such as the TMS in Washington, D.C., would present some challenges. Unlike the District of Columbia, the inner city of London exists and functions in a very small, geographically limited, self-contained area, which makes perimeter surveillance both feasible and reasonably secure. Enacting similar measures to achieve the same high degree of security confidence for the entire District of Columbia would be a challenging, if not overwhelming, task. The inner city of London also does not have a large population of permanent residents, and this has undoubtedly made public acceptance of the TMS easier to achieve. Automated surveillance systems could not operate as efficiently in the District of Columbia because of the far greater number of people that actually live in the

---

[6]Gearson and Freedman, 2000, pp. 21 and 25; Hardy, 1998.

District and its environs. Finally, the perceived threat of truck bombs is probably not as great in Britain as it is in the United States, because the PIRA has followed a pattern of targeting commercial buildings at night or on weekends, when they are mostly unoccupied, and has usually given prior warning. This has arguably allowed British government and security officials to accept a higher risk threshold than their counterparts in the United States, where, after the World Trade Center and Oklahoma City bombings—both of which occurred during working hours—concern over mass civilian casualties remains paramount. Finally, Britain has a *national* vehicle registration system, which facilitates immediate information retrieval from one centralized database. In the United States, there is no national motor vehicle registration. Each state has its own Department of Motor Vehicles, and given the large number of vehicles registered in the United States, expeditious identification of ownership and registration would be problematical.

PARIS

Contingencies in Paris are essentially defined by the *Vigipirate* plan, which was introduced following a wave of bombings that rocked the country in 1995. Between July and October of that year, Algerian Armed Islamic Group (GIA) terrorists, using bombs consisting of four-inch nails wrapped around camping-style cooking-gas canisters, killed eight persons and wounded more than 180 others. The targets were almost invariably public gathering places—e.g., the Paris metro (subway), popular tourist attractions, sidewalk cafes, and schools—which indicates that the attacks were calculated by the perpetrators to inflict wanton harm on ordinary bystanders and passersby. Under the counterterrorist plan, which was implemented immediately in response to the first attacks, some 32,000 soldiers, police, and customs officials were mobilized to check the identities and documents of nearly three million persons, 70,000 of whom were detained for further questioning.[7]

Vigipirate essentially involves a flexible seven-tiered strategy that allows countermeasures to be upgraded or downgraded according to

---

[7]Macintyre, 1995, 1996. See also "St. Michel Bomb: Islamist Connection 'Most Likely,'" 1995; and Berkhan, 1995.

the situation at hand, as determined from ongoing assessments of the terrorist threat. The plan was not based on worst-case scenarios, nor did it proceed from a presumed assumption that countermeasures cannot be rolled back or scaled down. Three areas are emphasized: protection of government buildings; securing of soft civilian targets such as schools and libraries; and mitigation of the potential threat of truck bombs.[8]

These objectives have been accomplished without closing down or sealing off major roads and thoroughfares in Paris—not even those immediately adjacent to the presidential residence. According to senior French counterterrorism intelligence officials, two elements have been critical in the plan's success to date: thorough penetration of GIA cells operating in France (the preeminent current terrorist threat) and limiting truck traffic within Paris's inner precincts by maintaining a de facto *cordon sanitaire* around the city's outer ring road.[9]

Again, however, it is not certain how easily these measures would translate to Washington, D.C., much less to a wider American context. Restricting vehicular traffic from the confines of the District of Columbia would not be commercially possible given the number of businesses and commercial outlets located in the downtown area. And while proactive intelligence gathering must be viewed as a critical component of any counterterrorism program, it is facilitated in Paris by the fact that French security officials are essentially confronting a single, known adversary—the GIA. In the United States, in contrast, potential threats could conceivably emanate from a broad range of antigovernment extremists, both domestic and foreign-based. Finally, as American counterterrorism officials have pointed out, although the street beside the French presidential palace remains open to traffic without restriction, the building itself is protected by a high perimeter wall and a considerable setback. It is also not open to the public.[10]

---

[8]Discussions with senior French counterterrorism officials, Paris, April 28, 2000. See also "Plan Vigipirate et Appel à la Vigilance," 1996; Sage and Raitberger, 1995; and "France Relaxes Anti-Terror Plan but Keeps Frontier Controls," 1996.

[9]Discussions with senior French counterterrorism officials, Paris, April 28, 2000.

[10]Discussion with a former senior FBI official responsible for counterterrorism, May 30, 2000.

Chapter Five

CONCLUSION

For most of the White House's 200 years, U.S. presidents have embraced the Jeffersonian principle of maintaining the Executive Mansion as the "People's House," keeping it as open and accessible to the public as possible. This tradition has created and preserved an image for American citizens and foreign visitors alike of the United States as an open society with an accessible form of government. These democratic attributes have been maintained for two centuries despite continuous changes in the security environment. The freedom and openness of the nation's capital thus reflect American democratic values and leadership worldwide, and as a result, the symbolism of the District of Columbia is far greater than that of other cities across the country. It is, in fact, a matter of national importance.

Because the closure of Pennsylvania Avenue projects an image of fortification that is at odds with the core values of an open and democratic society, potential options and alternatives to closure that would still provide appropriate security for the President and the White House deserve thoughtful consideration and careful evaluation. These include the following:

1. The section of Pennsylvania Avenue that runs in front of the White House could be bounded by a pair of pedestrian bridges constructed in such a way that they effectively prevent access to trucks, buses, and other large vehicles. This would maintain a largely unhindered traffic flow, with at least two lanes running in each direction, while providing a formidable barrier to vehicles that exceed defined height, width, and weight restrictions. These

bridges could be constructed in such a manner that they would provide the requisite security while maintaining actual as well as symbolic accessibility of the entire White House area.

2. Defensive modifications could be made to Pennsylvania Avenue itself. The midsection of the street could be reconstructed to incorporate a modified Jefferson bow that would curve northward, adding another 60 feet of standoff distance in front of the White House. Curbside lanes and parking could also be permanently eliminated, leaving what would in effect become a four-lane, no-stopping roadway.

3. Physical countermeasures could be further enhanced through the introduction of state-of-the-art detection technology, including video surveillance and in-road explosive-trace sensors. In addition, a dedicated and highly visible executive protection force could be established, a force perhaps possessing different skills, training, armaments, and organization from those of the current forces.[1] The added benefits of such a unit—especially its potential deterrent value—have not been fully appreciated.

All these measures could provide the President with an appropriate level of protection against catastrophic truck-bomb threats while holding to the principles of open access and unrestricted freedom of movement around our nation's most important historical landmarks. To be sure, none of the measures is foolproof, and all could conceivably be defeated by a determined suicide attack by a fanatically driven terrorist. The same caveat, of course, also applies to the entire spectrum of threats directed against the President. However, the issue here is not protection of the President from *all possible* contingencies; it is, rather, the enactment of appropriate security measures that address reasonable threat contingencies within the context of an acceptable level of risk.

---

[1]Current security practices around the White House appear to be specifically designed to minimize the imposing presence of a heavily guarded facility staffed by visibly well-armed guards. We are suggesting that a deliberately more visible and perhaps formidable security presence might be a reasonable tradeoff if an appropriately accompanying security architecture could be developed. In many capitals of democratic countries, security personnel stand guard around important public buildings, armed with submachine guns and wearing flak jackets or other armored vests. A highly visible, reconfigured security force at the Executive Mansion could enhance deterrence of potential attacks.

All open democratic societies must accept a certain threshold of risk—as does the President himself every time he ventures out in public. The goal in countering the range of potential threats to the White House should be to provide a level of protection that addresses plausible scenarios while preserving, to the greatest possible extent, the symbolic freedom of this national landmark. Striking such a balance will never be easy, particularly since many other federal government buildings in the District could also conceivably be targeted in any terrorist attack. However, while it is not reasonable to insist on blanket security around every possible terrorist target in the entire city, the measures implemented must provide reasonable security for specific persons and buildings.

Current security preparedness around the White House reflects a predilection on the part of law-enforcement officials to design security measures on the basis of worst-case scenarios and to maintain a vehicular-traffic-free "sanitized space" around the Executive Mansion. It also ignores the inherently dynamic nature of the counterterrorism response environment and its ability to develop new capabilities. Certainly the United States is better prepared to address the terrorist threat than it has ever been, as a result of the tremendously increased attention and budgets that have been devoted to this problem over the past six years. These considerations should be as much a factor in White House security decisionmaking as the reflexively embraced alarmism that is apparent in the nation's current counterterrorist planning.

QUESTIONNAIRE

1. What were the primary factors that were considered in the decision to close Pennsylvania Avenue?

Probes:

- What was the purpose of closing down Pennsylvania Avenue?

- What were the original decisionmaking processes?

  — Have these processes changed since the original decision was taken?

- Who were the decisionmakers?

  — Are these decisionmakers still in place?

- What groups were consulted and why?

2. Having taken the decision to close down Pennsylvania Avenue, was any thought given to assessing how long the avenue should stay closed?

Probes (if yes):

- What factors were considered?

- Are these factors still relevant to conditions and threat levels as they exist today?

- Has there, in fact, been a reexamination of the original decision?

- (Only if not answered) Has there been any serious assessment of whether the decision to close Pennsylvania Avenue has created different threats to the White House (such as mortar attacks from roof tops or contiguous access roads)?

Probes (if no):

- Why was there no consideration of this?
- Has any thought recently been given to creating a reassessment process?

    — If yes, why?

    — If no, why?

3. *In looking to the future, have any alternatives been examined other than the complete closure of Pennsylvania Avenue?*

Probes (if yes):

- What are the alternatives?
- Who evaluates these alternatives and their applicability?
- Can these alternatives be reasonably implemented in terms of cost and potential disruption?
- Were any public/interest groups consulted in developing and assessing these alternatives?

Probes (if no):

- Why have other alternatives not been considered?

4. *Broadening the focus from the White House to external physical security in general, have the responses of other major capital cities faced with serious terrorist threats been examined?*

Probes (if yes):

- Are these responses applicable to Washington, D.C.?
- (If applicable) Have any of the lessons from other major cities been incorporated into physical counterterrorist planning?

Probes (if no):

- Why have the experiences of other major capital cities not been considered?

5. In terms of threat perception, what is the greatest type of danger posed by terrorists to Washington, D.C., today?

Probes:

- How are threat assessments made (current threat perceptions/ worst-case scenarios)?

- Is the terrorist threat confronting Washington, D.C., today the same as it was when the decision was made to close down Pennsylvania Avenue?

- (If no):

  —Has it increased or decreased?

  —Has it changed in terms of level, type, or both?

  —How does the continued closure of Pennsylvania Avenue address this threat?

  —How do physical security measures incorporated at other federal buildings address this threat?

MAJOR SECURITY BREACHES PRIOR TO THE 1994 WHITE HOUSE SECURITY REVIEW

Helicopter Assault on the White House, February 17, 1974

On the night of February 17, 1974, Pfc. Robert K. Preston, an Army helicopter mechanic stationed at Fort Meade, Maryland, stole a helicopter from the Army base and flew it toward the White House complex. After receiving a complaint from a citizen that Preston had landed briefly in a trailer park near Jessup, Maryland, before taking off again, Maryland State Police scrambled two police helicopters in pursuit of the stolen aircraft. Preston flew the helicopter down the Baltimore-Washington Parkway toward downtown Washington, D.C., buzzing traffic along the parkway.[1] He passed over the Executive Mansion and hovered over the south lawn, briefly touching down before flying toward the Washington Monument. Because the Executive Protection Service (EPS) did not know who was piloting the aircraft and was unaware that it had been stolen from Fort Meade, no attempt was made to shoot it down. Preston hovered for five minutes at the monument grounds before flying to the White House, almost ramming one of the Maryland state helicopters that was pursuing him.

Meanwhile, the EPS, having been alerted that Preston had entered restricted airspace, turned on the White House floodlights.[2] As the

---

[1]Madden, 1974, pp. 1 and 50.

[2]U.S. Department of the Treasury, 1995c, p. 99.

helicopter made its second pass over the White House grounds, EPS agents opened fire, blasting the helicopter with shotgun and sub-machine-gun fire and forcing it down. Preston was immediately sub-dued by EPS and Metropolitan police officers and was treated for superficial shotgun wounds.[3] He was later sentenced by a court mar-tial to several years of hard labor and fined $2,400. In addition, his private pilot's license was revoked by the Federal Aviation Ad-ministration.[4]

White House Gate-Crashing Incident, December 25, 1974

On Christmas Day, 1974, a man later identified as Marshall Fields, dressed like an Arab and claiming to be carrying explosives, crashed his Chevrolet Caprice through the northwest gate of the White House on Pennsylvania Avenue. The gate was heavily damaged but failed to disable the car. After driving up to within 10 feet of the White House north portico, Fields got out of the car with what appeared to be explosives attached to his body. He removed black satchels from the car and placed them in front of him as he stood for the next four hours in front of the west wing of the White House, holding what ap-peared to be wires for the explosives he was allegedly carrying. Ac-cording to the EPS, Fields was not "neutralized" because the security forces believed he was carrying explosives and the President was not in the White House at the time. Fields's only request was to talk to the Pakistani Ambassador, and he demanded that his request be played over the Howard University radio station. After hearing that the request was announced on the radio station, Fields surrendered.[5] Security officials quickly apprehended him, and bomb-squad and fire officials moved in to remove the "explosives," which turned out to be flares.[6] Fields was sentenced to 18 months in jail for destruc-tion of property.[7]

---

[3]Madden, 1974, p. 50.

[4]Associated Press, 1974b, p. 10; United Press International, 1974, p. 34.

[5]Shabecoff, 1974, pp. 1 and 24.

[6]U.S. Department of the Treasury, 1995c, p. 93.

[7]Ibid., p. 50.

Plane Crash on the White House South Lawn, September 12, 1994

Shortly before midnight on September 11, 1994, Frank Eugene Corder stole an airplane from Aldino Airport in Churchville, Maryland, and flew it toward Washington, D.C. The airplane was first detected at 1:06 a.m. by FAA radar at Baltimore/Washington International Airport. At 1:44 a.m., the control tower at Reagan National Airport picked up the radar signal from Corder's airplane, which was now 6.5 miles north of the White House, flying at an altitude of 2,700 feet. Within the next three minutes, the airplane descended approximately 1,000 feet and turned directly south. It flew over Washington Circle and entered the protected airspace over the White House known as P-56. This no-fly zone extends from the White House to the Mall and from the Capitol to the Lincoln Memorial and can be entered only by authorized aircraft. The airplane banked left in a U-turn near the Washington Monument and headed straight toward the Executive Mansion. Descending rapidly, the plane passed over the Ellipse and crashed onto the White House lawn at approximately 1:49 a.m. The plane skidded across the lawn, struck a tree just west of the south portico, and crashed into the southwest corner of the Executive Mansion, below the President's bedroom.[8]

White House Shooting, October 29, 1994

On October 29, 1994, Francisco Martin Duran walked outside the fence in front of the White House, pulled a semiautomatic rifle out from under his trench coat, and began firing at the north face of the White House. After the initial burst of gunfire, he ran toward the Treasury Building, continuing to fire occasionally through the fence. When Duran paused to reload, he was tackled by a tourist and subdued with the help of two other citizens, who held him until the Secret Service Uniform Division arrived. Duran was able to fire at least 29 rounds before being subdued; 11 of those rounds struck the White House façade on the north side, and one bullet penetrated a window in the press briefing room in the west wing.[9]

---

[8]Department of the Treasury, 1995c, pp. 32–33.
[9]Ibid.

BIBLIOGRAPHY

BOOKS AND ACADEMIC JOURNAL ARTICLES

Bell, J. Bowyer. *The Irish Troubles: A Generation of Violence 1967–1992.* Dublin: Gill and Macmillan, 1993.

Ellis, John W. *Police Tactics and Planning for Vehicular Bombing: Prevention, Defense and Response.* Springfield, IL: Charles C. Thomas Publishers Ltd., 1999.

Ford, Franklin L. *Political Murder: From Tyrannicide to Terrorism.* Cambridge, MA, and London: Harvard University Press, 1985.

Glassner, Barry. *The Culture of Fear: Why Americans Are Afraid of the Wrong Things.* New York: Basic Books, 1999.

Hoffman, Bruce. "America and the New Terrorism: The American Perspective," *Survival*, Vol. 42, No. 2, Summer 2000, pp. 161–166.

Jenkins, Brian M. "Evaluating Security Against Terrorism," in Martin Shubik (ed.), *Risk, Organizations, and Society.* Boston: Kluwer Publishers, 1991, pp. 79–96.

Lesser, Ian, et al. *Countering the New Terrorism.* Santa Monica, CA: RAND, MR-989-AF, 1999.

Reeve, Simon. *The New Jackals: Ramzi Yousef, Osama bin Laden and the Future of Terrorism.* Boston: Northeastern University Press, 1999.

Simon, Steven, and Daniel Benjamin. "America and the New Terrorism," *Survival*, Vol. 42, No. 1, Spring 2000, pp. 59–75.

PUBLISHED REPORTS

Counterterrorism Threat Assessment and Warning Unit, National Security Division. *Terrorism in the United States 1997.* Washington, D.C.: U.S. Department of Justice, Federal Bureau of Investigation, 1998.

_____. *Terrorism in the United States 1998.* Washington, D.C.: U.S. Department of Justice, Federal Bureau of Investigation, 2000.

Hoffman, Bruce. *The World Trade Center Bombing, The Three Mile Island Intrusion and the Potential Threat to Nuclear Power Plants.* Santa Monica, CA: RAND, CT-106, March 1993.

National Capital Planning Commission. *Designing for Security in the Nation's Capital: A Report by the Interagency Task Force of the National Capital Planning Commission.* Washington, D.C.: National Capital Planning Commission, October 2001.

National Commission on Terrorism. *Countering the Changing Threat,* Washington, D.C.: National Commission on Terrorism, May 2000.

National Research Council (NRC). *Protecting Buildings from Bomb Damage.* Washington, D.C.: National Academy Press, 1985.

_____. *The Embassy of the Future: Recommendations for the Design of Future U.S. Embassy Buildings.* Washington, D.C.: National Academy Press, 1986.

Office of the Coordinator for Counterterrorism. *Patterns of Global Terrorism 1999.* Washington, D.C.: U.S. Department of State, Publication 10687, April 2000.

Terrorist Research and Analytical Center, Terrorism Section, Criminal Investigative Division. *FBI Analysis of Terrorist Incidents in the United States.* Washington, D.C.: U.S. Department of Justice, Federal Bureau of Investigation, 1984.

_____. *Terrorism in the United States, 1982–1992.* Washington, D.C.: U.S. Department of Justice, Federal Bureau of Investigation, 1993.

U.S. Department of the Treasury. *Environmental Assessment. Implementation of White House Security Review Vehicular Traffic Restriction Recommendations.* Washington, D.C.: Department of the Treasury, June 1997.

_____. Memorandum, "Department of Treasury's White House Review," May 1, 1995.

_____. Order 110-09, May 19, 1995.

_____. *Public Report of the White House Security Review.* Washington, D.C.: Government Printing Office. 1995.

U.S. Department of Transportation. *Analysis of Transportation Conditions After Traffic Restriction and Street Modifications in the Vicinity of the White House.* Washington, D.C.: Federal Highway Administration, June 1996.

U.S. General Services Administration and U.S. Department of State, in cooperation with the American Institute of Architects. *Balancing Security and Openness: A Thematic Summary of a Symposium on Security and the Design of Public Buildings, November 30, 1999.* Washington, D.C.: General Services Administration, Public Buildings Service, 2000.

U.S. Park Service. *The White House and President's Park: Comprehensive Design Plan and Final Environmental Impact Statement.* Washington, D.C.: Department of the Interior, September 1999.

UNPUBLISHED DOCUMENTATION

Burnham, Robert J. Statement before the U.S. House of Representatives Subcommittee on Oversight and Investigations, May 19, 1999, available at http//:www.fbi.gov/pressrm/congress/congress99/ epa.htm.

Elliot, C. L. "The Defense of Buildings Against Terrorism and Disorder. A Design Philosophy for the Construction of Ordinary Buildings and Installations to Resist Terrorism and Public Disorder." University of Southampton, unpublished M.Phil. thesis, 1986.

Freeh, Louis J. Statement for the record before the Senate Select Committee on Intelligence, January 28, 1998, available at http//:www.fbi. gov/pressrm/congress/congress98/threats.htm

Gearson, John, and Lawrence Freedman. "Financial Centres and the Terrorism Threat: The Case of the IRA's British Mainland Campaign." Paper delivered before the RAND/Oklahoma "Terrorism and Beyond: The 21st Century" International Conference, Oklahoma City, April 17–19, 2000.

Gunaratna, Rohan. "Impact of Access Control on Protective Security: Closure of Pennsylvania Avenue for Vehicular Traffic." St. Andrews, Scotland: Centre for the Study of Terrorism and Political Violence, May 2000.

Jenkins, Brian Michael. "Combatting Terrorism: Assessing the Threat." Testimony before the Subcommittee on National Security, Veterans Affairs, and International Relations, Committee on Government Reform, U.S. House of Representatives, October 20, 1999.

Martinez, Barbara J. Statement for the record before the U.S. House of Representatives Transportation and Infrastructure Committee, Subcommittee on Oversight, Investigations, and Emergency Management, June 9, 1999, available at http//:www.fbi.gov/pressrm/congress/congress99/comterr.htm.

Moynihan, Senator Daniel Patrick. "Resolved: A National Conversation on Terrorism Is in Order." Transcript of a speech delivered at GSA Design Award Ceremony, The Ronald Reagan Building and International Trade Center, March 25, 1999.

Strauchs, John J. Testimony before the House Committee on Government Reform and Oversight, House of Representatives, concerning the closing of Pennsylvania Avenue in the vicinity of the White House for security reasons, June 7, 1996.

NEWSPAPER AND MAGAZINE ARTICLES

Associated Press. "Architect Sees His Work Turn to Rubble." *The Washington Post*, April 24, 1995.

_____. "Copter Over White House Is Shot Down by Guards: Stolen Military Craft Lands on South Grounds—Pilot Being 'Interviewed' by Secret Service Agents." *The New York Times*, February 17, 1974.

_____. "Soldier Gets Year Term for Helicopter Incident." *The New York Times*, August 30, 1974.

"Banks Take Brunt of Bishops Gate Bomb." *The Daily Telegraph* (London), April 26, 1993.

Bearden, Milt, and Larry Johnson. "Don't Exaggerate the Terrorist Threat." *The Wall Street Journal*, June 15, 2000.

Bennett, Will. "Simple Bombs Improved but Lack Accuracy." *The Independent* (London), February 8, 1991.

Berkhan, Med. "Islamists: The Division of Europe." *Le Point* (Paris), September 2, 1995.

Brown, DeNeen L., and Saundra Torry. "D.C. Anxious About Impact of Pennsylvania Ave. Closing. Officials Ponder Cost to City, Business, Commuters." *The Washington Post*, May 22, 1995.

"Capital Comment: Bush Driving for Cabbie Vote." *Washingtonian Magazine*, April 2000.

Clymer, Adam. "Senator and Delegate Back Plan to Reopen Pennsylvania Avenue." *The New York Times*, September 26, 2000.

Connett, David. "IRA City Bomb Was Fertilizer." *The Independent* (London), May 28, 1992.

Editorial, "To Restore Pennsylvania Avenue." *The Washington Post*, September 28, 2000.

"Explosion in Oklahoma City." *The Washington Post*, April 20, 1995.

Fehr, Stephen C. "The Avenue: Architects Envision a Pedestrian Plaza." *The Washington Post*, June 3, 1995a.

_____. "D.C. Says No to Federal Parking Bans. Officials Respond to Residents' Fears They're Slowly Being Cut Off from Their Own City." *The Washington Post*, July 1, 1995b.

_____. "Norton Claims Clinton Backing: Reopening Pennsylvania Avenue Dependent on Assuring Safety." *The Washington Post*, September 26, 2000.

_____. "Promoting an Open-Avenue Policy. Leaders React to Anger About Barriers on Pennsylvania." *The Washington Post*, May 18, 1996.

_____. "Report on Pennsylvania Avenue Closing Hits a Dead End." *The Washington Post*, June 3, 1997.

Fehr, Stephen C., and Maryann Haggerty. "Barricades a Blow to Business. Downtown Pinched by Routing, Less Parking After Pennsylvania Ave. Closing." *The Washington Post*, May 28, 1995.

Fehr, Stephen C., and Hamil R. Harris. "Conversion to Be Delayed a Week." *The Washington Post*, June 14, 1995.

_____. "No Miracle on H Street: Morning's a Breeze, but Avenue Closing Jams Evening Rush Hour." *The Washington Post*, May 23, 1995.

Fehr, Stephen C., and Alice Reid. "No Avenue for Escape, U.S. Agrees Pennsylvania's Close Is Damaging Downtown." *The Washington Post*, June 7, 1996.

Forgey, Benjamin. "A Capital Under Security's Siege. Sen. Moynihan Calls for 'National Conversation.'" *The Washington Post*, April 17, 1999.

_____. "Cityscape: A Chance to Restore a Symbol of an Open Society." *The Washington Post*, September 30, 2000a.

_____. "Plan Would Reopen Pennsylvania Ave.: Cars-Only Restriction Is Security Precaution." *The Washington Post*, September 25, 2000b.

"France Relaxes Anti-Terror Plan but Keeps Frontier Controls." *Agence France-Presse*, January 11, 1996.

Gailey, Phil, "Access to White House Is Impeded by Dump Trucks in Security Move." *The New York Times*, November 25, 1983.

Goshko, John M., and Scott Bowles. "New Security Measures Ordered by President: Federal Facilities to Get Stricter Controls." *The Washington Post*, June 29, 1995.

Hardy, James. "City Gets Cameras That Can Spot Terrorists." *The Sunday Telegraph* (London), August 2, 1998.

Jackson-Han, Sarah. "Security Fears Force Closure of Pennsylvania Avenue Near White House." *Agence France-Presse*, May 20, 1995.

Labaton, Stephen. "Pilot's Exploit Rattles White House Officials." *The New York Times*, September 13, 1994.

_____. "Security Plan: Close Pennsylvania Avenue." *The New York Times*, May 10, 1995.

Lewis, Roger. "Shaping the City—Reopening Pennsylvania Avenue: Time to Take Down the Barriers." *The Washington Post*, October 4, 1997.

Macintyre, Benjamin. "French Police Seize Bombs and Rifles in Paris Dawn Raids." *The Times* (London), February 20, 1996.

_____. "Parisians Face Up to Security Failure." *The Times* (London), October 19, 1995a.

_____. "The Presidency Behind Closed Doors." *The Times* (London), May 27, 1995b.

Madden, Richard L. "Soldier Lands Helicopter on White House Lawn." *The New York Times*, February 18, 1974.

Milton, Cathy, Jimmy Burns, and Richard Lapper. "Shattered City Strives for Business as Usual." *The Financial Times* (London), April 13, 1992.

Moore, Arthur Cotton. "Letters to the Editor—Americas Avenue." *The Washington Post*, July 13, 1996.

Moore, Tony. "Buildings and Bombs!" *Intersec: The Journal of International Security*, Vol. 10, Issue 5, May 2000, pp. 166–168.

"Plan Vigipirate et Appel à la Vigilance." *Societe* (Paris), December 6, 1996, available at http://www.humanite.presse.fr/journal/1996.

Pyatt, Rudolph A., Jr. "On Pennsylvania Avenue, the Options Are Hardly a Choice." *The Washington Post,* May 8, 1996.

Reuters. "CIA Boss Predicts Huge Surge in World Terrorism." *The Times* (London), December 20, 1995.

_____. "New Security Steps Being Taken at White House After Shooting." *The New York Times,* March 17, 1984.

Rodgers, Peter. "City Bomb Claims May Reach £1bn." *The Independent* (London), April 14, 1992.

Rufford, Nicholas. "Prime Suspect: Who Masterminded the Rocket Attack on MO6 Headquarters." *Sunday Times* (London), September 24, 2000.

Sage, Adam, and Francois Raitberger. "France Acts to Combat Bombers." *The Australian* (Brisbane), September 12, 1995.

Schmidt, William E. "Delays Seen in London." *The New York Times,* April 13, 1992a.

_____. "One Dead, 40 Hurt as Blast Rips Central London." *The New York Times,* April 25, 1993.

_____. "With London Still in Bomb Shock, Major Appoints His New Cabinet." *The New York Times,* April 12, 1992b.

Schribman, David. "Concrete Barriers Installed at White House Gate." *The New York Times,* December 4, 1983.

Shabecoff, Phillip. "Intruder in Car Smashes White House Gate." *The New York Times,* December 26, 1974.

Smith, Elbert B. "Shoot-Out on Pennsylvania Avenue," *American History,* May/June 1998, available at http://the historynet.com.

Stevenson, Richard W. "I.R.A. Says It Placed Fatal Bomb; London Markets Rush to Reopen." *The New York Times,* 26 April 1993.

"St. Michel Bomb: Islamist Connection 'Most Likely.'" *Le Figaro* (Paris), July 27, 1995.

Tendler, Stewart.   "A Crude and Lethal Weapon to Thwart the Security Forces." *The Times* (London), February 8, 1991.

Times Staff. "White House Alert Explained." *The New York Times,* November 29, 1983.

United Press International. "Pilot's License Revoked." *The New York Times*, February 28, 1974.

Warnecke, John Carl. "A Pennsylvania Avenue for the People." *The Washington Post,* August 9, 1998.

INTERVIEWS

Robert Blitzer, McLean Virginia, May 30, 2000.

Gary Burch, Washington, D.C., May 24, 2000.

Tom Carey, Washington, D.C., May 30, 2000.

William T. Coleman, Washington, D.C., June 2, 2000.

Tom Convery, Ventura, California, June 6, 2000.

Timothy Coughlin, Washington, D.C., June 27, 2000.

Gary Hanney, Washington, D.C., May 30, 2000.

Jim Johnson, Washington, D.C., October 11, 2000.

Harvey Joyner, Washington, D.C., May 24, 2000.

John Perren, Washington, D.C., May 30, 2000.

David Perry, Washington, D.C., June 27, 2000.

James Rice, Washington, D.C., May 30, 2000.

Barbara Riggs, Washington, D.C., October 11, 2000.

Kenneth Sparks, Washington, D.C., June 27, 2000.

William H. Webster, Washington, D.C., June 8, 2000.